# Weave It!
# Quilt It!
# Wear It!

Mary Anne
Caplinger

That
Patchwork
Place®

## Dedication

To my husband, John, and my parents,
Harley and Ruth Mary Broeker Griggs, with love.

## Acknowledgments

Special thanks to:

John and our children, Mike and Julie, for

technical help with the computer;

Joan Jacobs Gaylord, for research and brainstorming sessions;

Christine Barnes, Bonnie Berlin, Susan I. Jones, and Barbara

Weiland, who contributed their work to this book;

Nancy Beuttel, Heather Hill Designs, Boone, North Carolina,

for the use of her serger;

Richelle W. Ford, Quilt Soft, San Diego, California, for

Quilters' Design Studio software;

My editor, Barbara Weiland, for her guidance;

That Patchwork Place, for giving me the opportunity to take

this unexpected turn in my career.

## Credits

Editorial Director . . . . . . . . . . . . . . . . . . . . . . . . . . . . . Kerry I. Hoffman
Technical Editor . . . . . . . . . . . . . . . . . . . . . . . . . Barbara Weiland
Managing Editor . . . . . . . . . . . . . . . . . . . . . . . . . . . . . . . Greg Sharp
Text and Cover Design . . . . . . . . . . . . . . . . . . . . . . Joanne Lauterjung
Copy Editors . . . . . . . . . . . . . . . . . . . . . . . . . . . . . . . . Liz McGehee
　　　　　　　　　　　　　　　　　　　　　　　　 Sherri Schultz
Proofreader . . . . . . . . . . . . . . . . . . . . . . . . . . . . . . . Melissa Riesland
Production Assistants . . . . . . . . . . . . . . . . . . . . . . . Dani Ritchardson
　　　　　　　　　　　　　　　　　　　　　　　 Claudia L'Heureux
Technical Illustrator . . . . . . . . . . . . . . . . . . . . . . . . . . . . Laurel Strand
Fashion Illustrator . . . . . . . . . . . . . . . . . . . . . . . . . . . . . . . . Jill Kelto
Photography . . . . . . . . . . . . . . . . . . . . . . . . . . . . . . . . . . . Brent Kane
Models . . . . . . . . . . . Kathy Culley, Monica Doramus, Kerry I. Hoffman,
　　　　　　　 Valerie McConnaughey, Lisa McKenney, Donna Pritchard

Weave It! Quilt It! Wear It!
© 1996 by Mary Anne Caplinger
That Patchwork Place, Inc., PO Box 118, Bothell, WA 98041-0118 USA

Printed in the United States of America
01 00 99 98 97 96　　6 5 4 3 2 1

**Library of Congress Cataloging-in-Publication Data**

Caplinger, Mary Anne
　　Weave it! Quilt it! Wear it! / by Mary Anne Caplinger.
　　　　p.　cm.
　　Includes bibliographical references.
　　ISBN 1-56477-142-3
　　1. Patchwork—Patterns.　2. Strip quilting—Patterns.　3. Hand weaving.
　　4. Quilted goods.　5. Wearable art.　I. Title.
TT835.C367　　1996
746.46'0432—dc20　　　　　　　　　　　　　　　　　95-48409
　　　　　　　　　　　　　　　　　　　　　　　　　　　　CIP

# CONTENTS

## CHAPTER 1
## The Key Ingredients: Color, Fabric & Style

## CHAPTER 2
## Tools & Supplies

## CHAPTER 3
## Weaving & Quilting Basics

## CHAPTER 4
## Garment Cutting, Assembly & Finishing

## CHAPTER 5
## Three Sample Projects

## CHAPTER 6
## Design Portfolio

## CHAPTER 7
## Lagniappe

## CHAPTER 8
## Weaving Patterns

## Appendix

# Clothing—Our Visual Language

All of us have an identity through associations. If you open your wallet and spread your credit cards, pictures, and identification cards on a table before me, I can put together pieces of information about you based on your family relationships and your membership in certain organizations.

For example, your Sierra Club membership indicates that you care deeply about the environment, your PTA card identifies you as a parent of a school-age child, and your driver's license demonstrates that you have met your state's requirements for operating a motor vehicle.

In this book, we'll be looking at an identity we have through a different kind of association—the clothing we wear. Instead of sorting through written information on small cards, we'll be looking at equally revealing combinations of color, shape, and texture in our clothes. These clues are more subtle, but we can learn to read the visual language as easily as we read alphabetical characters on a page.

"What are you going to wear?" is a common question even today, when the rules of "proper dress" are relaxed and sometimes only a difference in size distinguishes a toddler's clothes from her grandmother's. It's always unsettling to arrive at an event and find you've worn inappropriate clothes. Most of us would rather not dress exactly like someone else, yet each of us wants to be within a range of acceptability.

Close friends and co-workers may know our hobbies, our politics, and our favorite foods, but everyone we meet forms an opinion about us from observing our clothes. In the space of a few seconds, our choice of colors and styles shows our personality, our mood, and possibly our profession.

Does clothing really matter that much? Are we always judged by seemingly superficial standards? Humans are social by nature and thrive on recognition by their peers. The clothes we wear are a visible sign of the place in society that we've chosen for ourselves. So, since we have to wear clothes, why not have fun with them and show our passion for fibers and fabrics at the same time?

In recent years, products and techniques for sewing our own clothes have improved dramatically. No longer do we have to settle for the "loving hands at home" look. Attitudes are also changing as people realize that most women and men who sew their own clothes do so because they want to express their creativity while getting good fit and value for their time and money.

By joining the work of our heart, mind, and hands, we can write our own version of an identification card using visual language. Individual combinations of color, line, and technique, blended with contemporary styling, produce distinctive clothing that is truly wearable and identifies you as a creative, imaginative individual with your very own style.

# How to Use This Book

As I discussed in the preface to my first book, *Woven and Quilted*, I developed my technique for creating the look of patchwork because I wanted to eliminate the struggle of cutting and precisely matching hundreds of small fabric pieces. On a chance visit to a friend's home, I noticed a color study of woven construction paper hanging in her sewing room. As the wheels in my mind started turning, I wondered if I could do the same thing with fabric. I couldn't wait to get home and experiment!

Obviously it worked, because here I am writing a second book on the subject, this time devoting the pages to a thorough discussion of how to use my woven and quilted techniques to create one-of-a-kind garments that you will be proud to wear.

The technique discussed in this book is easy and versatile. It will enable you to quickly create several interesting pieces to add to your wardrobe.

The chapters in this book guide you in the process of making a unique garment. Use the book as a reference and a workbook for visualizing your concepts. The first chapter contains information and suggestions for choosing colors, fabrics, and a flattering pattern style for woven and quilted clothing. The tools and supplies you'll need for planning, measuring, and constructing woven and quilted yardage are detailed in the second chapter.

The third chapter describes the basic weaving process. You'll learn to read a weaving diagram and have fun charting your personal color choices on the blank grids included in the Appendix on pages 80–84. You'll find out how to select the right backing and batting and how to prepare your fabric. Step-by-step directions show you how to weave and quilt the yardage for each piece of the garments you wish to make.

Woven and quilted garments require some special sewing techniques. These are discussed in Chapter Four, "Garment Cutting, Assembly & Finishing." Be sure to read the "Problem Solving" section at the end of the chapter. There you will find the answers to specific design and construction challenges that you may encounter when planning and making a woven and quilted garment.

In Chapter Five, you will find complete step-by-step directions for three different garments—two simple vests and a coat. If you learn best by doing, I suggest you read the first four chapters in this book, then make the vest "Summer Dreamin' " on pages 38–43 to start your first weaving project, referring often to the basics in Chapter Three.

For inspiration before you start your first garment, browse through "Chapter Six: Design Portfolio" on pages 51–65. You will see a wide array of interesting garments, some featuring small sections embellished with the woven and quilted technique, as well as entire coats and jackets cut from woven and quilted yardage. These vests, jackets, and coats, from casual to one-of-a-kind artwear, show the versatility of the woven and quilted technique.

Chapter Seven includes a number of exciting ways to take the woven and quilted concept to new heights of creativity in garments.

Chapter Eight includes examples of many types of weaves to explore with fabric strips. Diagrams are presented in black and white and in color to spark your creative juices.

The Appendix contains blank weaving diagrams and viewfinders to use as you plan your woven and quilted garment.

So, gather your colored pencils and scissors, find a comfortable place to work, and let your imagination take off as you design an outstanding and innovative piece of wearable art.

*Mary Anne*

## CHAPTER 1

# The Key Ingredients: Color, Fabric & Style

Whenever you make a garment, you must consider color, fabric, and style and how they will work together in the completed garment. In addition, you must take care that the combination works on your body type and with your coloring.

## MAKING COLOR WORK FOR YOU

Color is the magic ingredient in every garment you make. It's a very personal choice, and it's the one that will have more visual impact than any other element of the finished garment. Working with fabric in a color you love can ease you through a frustrating technical process. Wearing a garment in a flattering color lifts your spirits and rewards you for the time spent making it. Understanding color dynamics helps you make color choices that will enhance your woven and quilted garments.

When choosing colors for woven and quilted clothing (or any clothing, for that matter), remember that colors are always seen in relation to each other. For example, the red swatch in the illustration below looks warm when placed next to the green, and cool when it's next to the orange.

You can apply this principle when selecting clothing colors. The color of your clothes should relate to the colors of your surroundings, especially your hair, skin, and eye colors.

For example, the beautiful red silk dress displayed in the store window is an illusion of color and sheen. The moment you it slip on, it changes from just a red dress to a red dress seen next to the color of your skin, your hair, your eyes, and the quality of light in your environment. The particular shade and tone of the red silk fabric must harmonize with your coloring and your environment for it to look truly beautiful on you.

One well-known system for organizing the relationship between personal coloring and clothing colors uses the colors found in nature during each season as a guide for choosing wardrobe colors. Investigate some of the currently popular color and image books to become more aware of the effects of different colors in clothes and makeup. Analyze the undertone in your skin color, in a range from blue to yellow, to find your favorite shade or tone that harmonizes well with your coloring. See the bibliography on page 87.

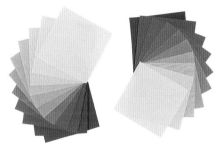

*Everyone can wear red! Drape red fabrics, matching several colors along the continuum of warm or cool reds, to find the ones that light up your features. Is your personal coloring cool or warm?*

The geographical area of the world where you live also influences your color and fabric choices for clothing. Hot pink, bright orange, and chartreuse green are natural in a tropical environment, but they look shrill and garish in a cool, foggy city. In contrast, muted versions of the same colors fit well in a gentle country setting.

Use color in your woven and quilted clothing to highlight your best features. For most of us, that means placing light or bright colors closer to the face and away from the midsection of the body. These colors become a focal point, drawing attention to your most lively and

animated features. Using the same principle to accent a small waistline, you could make a belt in light or bright colors to contrast with the main color of your dress.

Clever placement of color can also camouflage areas of your figure that you don't want to emphasize. A light color in the shoulder area contrasted with a dark color on your hips will visually widen the shoulders and decrease the hips. This is easy to do when making a woven top because you can control the color of the weft strips, those that will go across the body when the garment pieces are cut from the completed yardage.

For example, to make a vest using this principle of camouflage, select dark fabric for the warp (vertical strips), then shade the weft (horizontal strips) from light to dark, beginning at the shoulders. You will have a checkerboard effect at the top that moves down into a textured dark solid at the bottom. The high-contrast checkerboard will be the focal point at the shoulders, and the eye will skim over the lower portion of your vest.

*Far left: Bold, bright colors and prints remain true under the glare of strong sunlight.*
*Left: Delicate, subtle tints reflect the soft light found in regions farther from the equator.*

The successful balance between the color and the shape of a garment is subtle. Fashion magazines and runway shows often feature clothes in exaggerated shapes and bright colors to create an exciting and dramatic production. You can learn some tricks of the trade from these avant-garde fashions by noting the placement of accent colors and attention-getting details.

A survey of current fashion magazines will demonstrate the power of color to create interest in a specific area of a garment. For example, a quilted jacket in gold lamé, accented with large, shiny black studs, will not work in all wardrobes, but that idea might translate into small appliquéd circles on the yoke of a woven and quilted cotton jacket.

# CHOOSING SUITABLE FABRICS

Dreaming about, collecting, and working with beautiful fabrics is the reason most of us are attracted to quilting and sewing. We touch each piece of cloth, mentally imagining it in a quilt or garment. We analyze the weight and drape for the best use of that fabric. Is it firmly woven, smooth textured, and medium weight—perfect for a wall quilt that hangs straight and flat? Softer fabrics that scrunch into a cozy wrap make an inviting bed quilt. Many garment styles require softer fabrics to drape around our curves and move when we do.

One of the joys of the woven and quilted process is the freedom it gives you to use different kinds of fabrics. The technique doesn't require precision piecing or hand-stitched appliqué. Instead, it frees you to choose from a wider range of fabrics for woven and quilted yardage.

Because the woven and quilted process mimics weaving on a loom, fabric weight becomes an important factor. In traditional weaving, each weft yarn goes over and under the warp yarns in a prescribed fashion. Wherever they cross, there is a double layer of yarn. The same is true for woven and quilted yardage. Wherever the fabric strips cross each other, there is a double layer of fabric.

The double layers make weight the first consideration when selecting suitable fabrics for woven and quilted garments. Lightweight cottons are fine, but you can also use thin, sheer, or fragile fabrics that usually don't work for traditional piecing techniques. That opens the door to a greater variety of beautiful fabrics of varying fiber contents.

If you have concentrated on collecting quilting cottons in the past, now is the time to stretch those boundaries and investigate other fibers and fabrics. Some fabrics such as wool challis and many fabrics made of rayon or lightweight silk are called transitional or seasonless because they work so well in all climates. These are good choices for woven and quilted garments because they

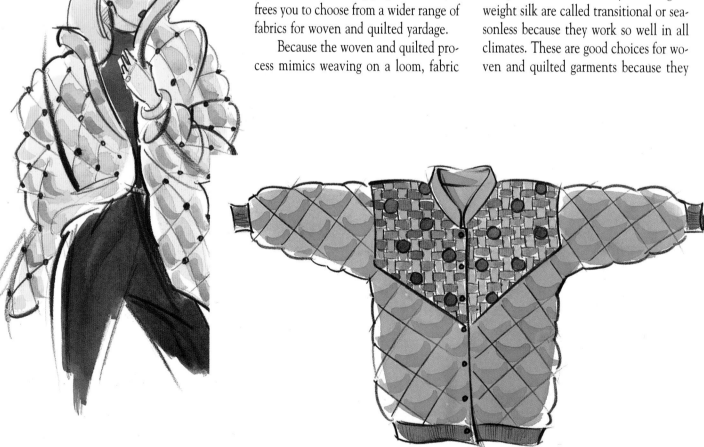

are lightweight. A touch of linen, silk, or wool will flow easily into a woven and quilted garment and perk up your wardrobe too.

Inspiration for your color and fabric choices can come from many sources. You might begin with a small length of silk fabric from your collection as the basis for a lovely dressy jacket for a special occasion. A scavenger hunt to collect several other fabrics in similar colors will get you started and may become part of the story surrounding the making of the jacket. To unify a mix of textured fabric in different weights, stay within a single color family.

Monochromatic (mono = one; chroma = color) color schemes are a good choice for clothes to wear to work. Career clothing is perhaps the most difficult area in which to express your creativity because, in many industries, your work clothes must be tailored and understated. Subtle, muted colors in smooth-surfaced, natural-fiber fabrics combined with classic garment shapes give you an original look while still conforming to the workplace norms. Neutrals—beige, khaki, navy blue, or black—in cotton, linen, or lightweight wool are another possibility.

Plans for a vacation trip might motivate you to make new clothes. Perhaps you're traveling to a different area of the country and need some casual clothes for sightseeing. For a sightseeing trip to Florida, perk up a basic sundress with a new woven and quilted pocket in tropical colors.

Winter holidays provide a great incentive for adding a new garment to your wardrobe. Consider adding a touch of glitz to the traditional reds and greens associated with the season.

*Consider a variety of fabric types and fiber contents for woven and quilted projects.*

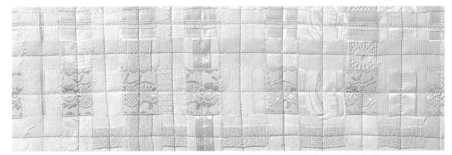

*An elegant evening jacket made in a combination like this one, including off-white silks, rayons, woolens, and polyesters, can be worn year 'round.*

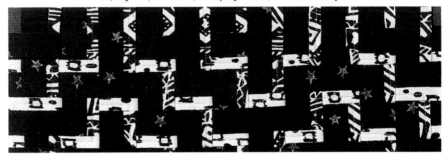

*A woven and quilted vest made of black-and-white prints would be versatile and appropriate for many offices or classrooms.*

*Lemons, limes, and oranges might look refreshing in a summer dress.*

*A simple vest in traditional colors takes on a new dimension with the addition of mega-stitching in shiny rayon and metallic threads.*

You may also want to experiment with ideas for color combinations that you've seen in a photograph or a natural object such as a rock or a leaf. Select fabrics in light, medium, and dark colors that match the colors in your source. With fabrics in hand, you can try to use the colors in the same proportions as those in your source of inspiration, or you can choose to focus on one area.

For example, a photo of the Golden Pavilion in Kyoto, Japan, served as the inspiration for a sample weaving that emphasizes the trees and water at the scene. Neutrals from the building in the photo became accents in the weaving.

The woven and quilted technique gives you a wonderful opportunity to play with colors on the surface of a quilted garment. It's fun to watch the effect develop as you experiment with simple two-color checkerboard designs in cottons and then move on to more elaborate weaving patterns, such as a twill weave made with many colors and textured fabrics. The colors and prints in each combination of fabrics will surprise you as they interact, forming a new design. Because you are creating a new surface from one or more fabrics, you can control the color sequence, the shading, and the amount of texture.

The diagrams that illustrate weave structures in Chapter Eight show how you can choose colors and fabrics to emphasize or downplay the weave structure. To highlight the weave structure, use two contrasting colors, such as black and white, or two fabrics with contrasting textures, such as a shiny silk and a matte-surface cotton. As you increase the number of colors or textures, the weave structure itself becomes less noticeable. "Weaves with Special Effects" on pages 77–79 shows some fascinating ways to manipulate color and fabric choices independent of the weave structure.

A vacation memory translated in fabric

# SELECTING A PATTERN

Matching your chosen colors and fabrics to a stylish pattern is the next step in planning a garment.

It's worth spending time in a store trying on several clothing styles before you plan your new garment because when you find a flattering shape, you can repeat it often in different colors and textures. Study the relationship of the garment parts to each other, just as you consider color relationships when choosing your fabrics. Notice how each style affects the perceived proportion of your torso to your legs, and the symmetry between your shoulders and hips. Select a garment style that provides a pleasing, but not equal, balance between the upper and lower portions of your body.

When selecting a pattern, there are three important points to remember:

• Quilted fabrics are stiffer and bulkier than the single layer of fabric in most clothing. A stiff fabric requires tailoring to fit smoothly over body curves. This could mean selecting a vest with darts or a

jacket with set-in rather than dolman sleeves. Some patterns are designed specifically for quilted fabrics. Look for designs illustrated in quilted fabrics. If possible, select a pattern from this group for the basic shape of your garment and add details from other sources. Examine these styles carefully for hints on style lines to look for in other pattern designs. Be sure to read the suggested fabric list on the back of the pattern envelope. If the pattern is suitable for heavier fabrics, it will probably work for your woven and quilted yardage.

In some garments, two or more fabrics are combined for contrast and interest—for example, a contrasting yoke or collar and cuffs on a jacket. If you don't wish to make an entire garment of woven and quilted fabric, make small amounts to use for contrast in these areas. Be careful when planning contrasting areas so that the resulting garment is not spotty and distracting. Adding interest in one or three areas (such as a yoke or a collar and both cuffs) is more successful than adding interest to only two areas (such as only the

cuffs) or more than three areas in the garment. Don't get carried away. When in doubt, less is best.

Semi-fitted to loose-fitting (but not too loose-fitting) jackets, vests, and coats with minimal, straight seaming, few or no darts, and simple set-in sleeves are the best pattern choices for woven and quilted yardage. A cut-on sleeve (such as a dolman) may work if you are weaving with very lightweight fabrics, as in the chiffon jacket shown on page 60. Embellishments, such as those shown on some of the garments in the "Design Portfolio" on pages 51–65, add interest to otherwise simple shapes. In addition, consider making the body of a garment (such as a jacket) from your woven and quilted yardage, then cutting the sleeves from one of the fabrics you used in the weaving. That way, you can use a style with a softer, less structured sleeve if you wish. Examine the garments featuring this design idea in the "Design Portfolio."

• Fabrics with an unusual surface design and texture look best in a gar-ment with a simple shape and un-cluttered lines. Woven and quilted yardage is not appropriate for a style with pleats and ruffles or many design details. Using textured fabrics for this sort of style would confuse the focus of your garment and create sewing problems.

• You are three-dimensional! You may choose to put the focal point on the front or back of your garment, but don't isolate it. The fronts, back, sleeves, collar, and front or back openings should work together for a cohesive look.

# Design sketchbook

Pattern on inset yoke of dress

yoke + top of sleeves

of jacket 'ress

Red wool jacket — detachable collar of woven black ribbons — edge the collar with the sequin trim

Suit of natural silk noil — add attachable collar on one side as in illustration ...ld metallic

Weave... for b...

Short jacket—
mix of madras plaids,
denim — piping
around neck edge
and sleeve edges

denim
dress

Weave the bib top—
leave pocket plain?
or counterchange?

skirt & straps

HOG WASH

Vest is attached
to the front only

Red silk pangee
for dress

Vest black China silk
with strips of
bright print

# CHECKING THE FIT—MAKING A MUSLIN

The appearance and longevity of your clothes depend on proper fit. All clothes should have enough wearing ease to allow every seam to hang smoothly. If a seam is pulled so tightly that the stitches show, the garment needs adjusting to prevent a rip. Undesirable wrinkles and creases also indicate improper fit. In addition, avoid fitting the garment with too much fullness. Woven and quilted yardage will not hang in loose folds, so a loose-fitting style will overwhelm you.

In preparing to make a garment using woven and quilted yardage, it's best to ensure a good fit by making a test garment, or "muslin," as it is commonly called, using an inexpensive fabric. Making a muslin allows you to perfect the fit and try on a new style, or combine elements from different patterns with a minimum of preparation.

Called a "muslin," regardless of the actual fabric used, the sample saves time and money. You cut and pin until the fit is correct, then transfer the changes to the pattern before cutting it from your woven and quilted yardage.

To make your muslin, select an inexpensive fabric similar in weight and drape to your fashion fabric. Look for bargains in the sale corner or on the flat-fold tables in your local fabric store. Cut and baste together the major pieces of the garment, slip in a pair of shoulder pads if required, then try it on for fit in front of a full-length mirror. Analyze the drape and placement of seam lines at the sides and back as well as the front. Using a hand mirror, look at the back view to check the fit across the shoulders and hips. After fitting the muslin to your figure, take it apart and transfer all the changes to the paper pattern for a permanent reference.

For example, if you are making a woven and quilted jacket or coat:

1. Cut the back, fronts, and sleeves from plain prequilted cotton. Mark and stitch any darts or pleats first, then machine baste the shoulder, sleeve, and side seams. If you're unsure about the collar, lapels, or pockets, baste them in place also. Pin the shoulder pads in place. Check the fit in a full-length mirror and make the necessary adjustments. Shown below are three easy alterations you may need to make to fit a jacket, coat, or vest.

2. Transfer any alterations you made in the muslin to your paper pattern. The pattern piece must lie flat after the alterations are made. If you have pinned or slashed the fabric, continue the alteration lines all the way to the outside edge of the pattern piece as shown.

If you are unfamiliar with the fitting process and wish to learn more, there are two good books on fitting listed in the bibliography on page 87.

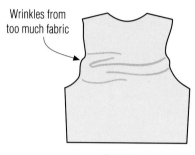

Wrinkles from too much fabric

Erect Back

Pin the extra fabric into a horizontal tuck, tapering out to nothing at the pattern edge.

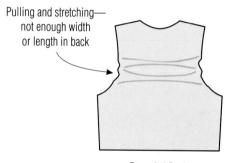

Pulling and stretching—not enough width or length in back

Rounded Back

Slash pattern and add extra inches for ease.

Sloping Shoulders

Increase depth of shoulder seam, tapering to nothing at neckline. Recut armhole seam if necessary.

# Tools & Supplies

## PLANNING AIDS

The proper work surface and a few tools and supplies will speed your weaving and help you create straight, neat pieces of woven and quilted yardage. Before you begin, assemble the following planning aids:

- Colored pencils
- Two small mirrors for enlarging a weaving diagram
- Photocopies of the weaving blanks in the Appendix (pages 85–86)
- White paper for making a viewfinder (pages 18–19)
- Graph paper
- Commercial clothing pattern(s)

A collection of planning aids

## WORK SURFACES

In the traditional weaving process, warp threads are held on a loom under tension while the weft threads are woven under and over them. Even though you won't be threading your fabric strips on a loom, you'll need to hold them taut. Choose one of the following alternative work surfaces for your weaving:

**Table.** You can use any flat tabletop for weaving. In my workshops, two people usually share an 8-foot Formica®-top table. For proper tension, we secure the fabric to the tabletop with masking tape. If you need to work on a good kitchen or dining room table, cover it with cardboard or layers of newspaper to prevent accidental pin pricks. Lay an extra-long piece of muslin over the cardboard or newspapers; wrap the fabric to the underside of the table and tape it in place.

**Collapsible cardboard cutting table.** This table, 32" x 55", is my favorite surface for working on woven projects because I can stick pins directly into the tabletop. It's easy to adjust the tension or change strips during weaving. The table is lightweight and has removable legs, allowing you to store work in progress. You can order the table with legs that are 34" or 40" long; choose the height that's most convenient for you. See "Resources" on page 87.

**Work-space board.** An alternative to using a separate table is a work-space board. This surface is a large heat- and water-resistant board covered with cotton fabric printed in a 1" grid. The board folds in half for easy storage of a work in progress. The large size, 33" x 51", covers an average dining room table. The junior size, 21" x 27", packs conveniently for a class. See "Resources" on page 87.

**Quilt frame.** You can also use a traditional floor quilt frame for weaving. Attach the backing and batting as usual, then pin the warp strips to the batting at the top of the frame. You'll need to experiment to determine how to pin the other ends of the warp strips for the necessary tension. You may need to complete the top half of your project, roll it on the frame, and then continue working on the lower half.

**Pressing surface.** A portable pressing pad, 13" x 14", is just the right size for small weaving projects. One side is a rotary-cutting mat; the other has a cushion marked with a 1" grid.

## MEASURING, MARKING & CUTTING TOOLS

If you choose to tear your fabric strips, you'll need a tape measure and scissors for measuring and marking the fabric. If you cut your strips, you'll need a rotary cutter, mat, and ruler.

**Rotary cutter.** A rotary cutter looks like a pizza cutter with a protective shield for the blade. Rotary cutters are available in three sizes. Many prefer the two larger sizes because they feel it's easier to cut through several layers of fabric at a time with a large blade. Rotary cutters have extremely sharp blades. Never leave the blade exposed, even for a moment. Rotary cutters with manually engaged safety shields are the best. Get in the habit of engaging the safety shield as soon as you finish each cut. Automatically re-tracting safety shields are not as safe because the shield may retract when dropped or touched.

**Rotary mat.** A self-healing rotary mat protects both the blade and the work surface. Mats come in several sizes; choose the most convenient size for your work surface. The 32" x 55" mat fits the top of the collapsible cardboard cutting table. Although expensive, this mat is a good investment.

**Rotary rulers.** These rulers come in different sizes and grid for-mats. Compare the marks and colors on various rulers to see which you prefer. For woven and quilted projects, it's helpful to have a ruler that is at least 5" x 24". Use this to check the alignment of the fabric strips while weaving.

**Markers.** Chalk is best for marking warp and weft guidelines.

A collection of measuring and construction tools

# WEAVING & SEWING TOOLS

**Weaving needles.** You may find that weaving by hand is easy and fun. You may, however, prefer a flat weaving needle or a long craft needle with a large eye, the kind used in dollmaking.

You can also make a satisfactory needle from a clean plastic milk carton. Cut a strip approximately 1" x 5"; taper one end and cut a 1" slit close to the opposite end for the eye. Lightly sand the edges.

**Pins.** Very fine, glass-head silk pins are the easiest to slide through the layers of fabric.

**Fusible web.** Paper-backed fusible web allows you to change strips in the middle of a row. Follow the manufacturer's in-structions carefully. See "Changing Strips in Mid-row" on page 26.

**Iron.** A good steam iron makes pressing the fabric strips fast and easy. You'll also need your iron for fusing strips.

**Seam roll.** Place this oblong form, filled with sawdust, under seam lines to press without leaving impressions from the seam allowances.

**Sewing machine.** Have your machine in good working order before you begin; remove any lint, oil if necessary, and ad-just the tension discs.

**Thread.** For sewing, use polyester or cotton/polyester thread on the machine. To add visual excitement to your quilting, experiment with rayon, silk, and metallic threads. For less obvious quilting, use sewing thread in a matching color.

**Needles.** For machine quilting, a medium-size (85 or 11) uni-versal-point needle will usually go through the layers of fabric and batting easily. Consider the thread you will be using and select an appropriate needle. Special machine-embroidery needles and needles designed for metallic threads are available.

If your machine begins to skip stitches, try a needle made especially for quilting; it has a very sharp point and a larger eye. You can also use a stretch needle, which is longer than a regular needle and has an antistatic coating. Another option is a jeans needle, which has a very fine, sharp point. Both stretch and jeans needles come in a vari-ety of sizes.

For hand quilting, you may wish to experiment with a larger-size needle than you normally use because you'll be quilting through an extra layer of fabric. If you still have difficulty quilting, try using a needle lubricant.

**Masking tape.** Use masking tape to anchor the backing and batting to your work surface before you begin weaving.

## CHAPTER 3

# Weaving & Quilting Basics

## WEAVING TERMS

Two words used in this book may not be familiar to you—"warp" and "weft." If you look closely at a piece of cotton shirting or quilting fabric with a magnifying glass, you'll be able to distinguish two perpendicular sets of threads.

*Warp.* The lengthwise threads, parallel to the selvage edges of finished cloth, are called the warp. The warp threads are attached to the loom during weaving. Because these threads are strong and stable, most fabric pieces for clothing are cut with the warp running vertically, also known as the lengthwise grain.

When torn along the lengthwise grain, many fabrics stretch and have long threads along the resulting raveled edge. If you wish to use a fabric with a vertical design, it's best to *cut* the strips rather than tear them.

*Weft.* The horizontal threads that run from selvage to selvage are called the weft, also known as the cross grain. In the weaving process, the weft threads are interlaced with the warp threads to form cloth. If you hold a piece of fabric with one selvage in each hand and stretch it, you'll see that the weft threads are slightly more elastic than the warp. Most of the projects in this book were made with strips of fabric that were torn on the cross grain—that is, from selvage to selvage.

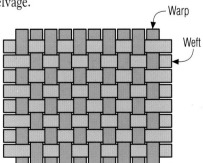

*Bias.* Bias refers to any diagonal line that intersects the lengthwise and crosswise threads (the warp and weft). When fabric is cut on the true bias (at a 45° angle to the selvage), it

has maximum elasticity and doesn't ravel much. You can cut on the bias to take advantage of a particular design. For example, stripes and other vertical designs gain energy and movement when cut on the bias. See page 21 for a woven sample using fabrics cut on the bias.

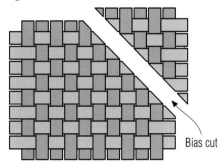

Bias cut

## A SAMPLE WEAVING DIAGRAM

The diagram below shows a sample weaving sequence in plain weave using ten different fabrics for the warp and weft. To make the weaving diagrams easy to read, there are small spaces between the warp and weft strips. In an actual weaving, the edges of the strips would be right next to each other to prevent the underlayer of batting (or lining fabric) from showing.

The weaving sequence for each garment in this book is illustrated in the same way. The fabrics are indicated by different colors, or black and white.

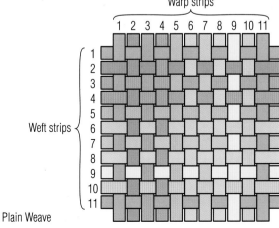

Plain Weave

To read the weaving diagram, follow a warp strip from top to bottom, noting how often it goes over and under a weft strip. Then look at the adjacent warp strips to see if they follow the same sequence. Next, trace the path of a weft strip from one side to the other. Follow its adjacent strips, again noting the sequence.

For example, in the plain weave diagram on page 17, each warp strip goes over one weft and under the next. Each weft strip also goes over one warp and under the next, producing a balanced weave. In more complicated weaving patterns, such as twill, a warp strip may go over two or more weft strips and then go under the same number or a different number of weft strips. For easier reading, I often use a ruler or a piece of white paper to underline the rows.

Twill Weave

Look around your home at the objects you use every day. You may be surprised to recognize weaving patterns in unexpected sources, such as baskets, rugs, wicker furniture, and even shoes. Read these weaving patterns as you did the diagrams above, tracing the path of a warp strip and a weft strip to see the relationship between them.

# Planning a Weaving Colorway

To experiment with your own choices of color and weaving patterns, use the blank weaving diagrams in the Appendix on pages 80–84. Photocopy a diagram and fill in the rows with colored pencils. Begin coloring one warp row near the center at the top. Follow that row straight down, filling ten or twelve spaces. Then move to adjacent warp rows, changing colors as desired. Next, begin coloring weft rows. You will see the pat-

tern emerging as you complete ten or twelve rows of weft. Stop at this point and analyze the diagram. Hold two small mirrors at right angles to the colored diagram to see it multiplied and as mirror images.

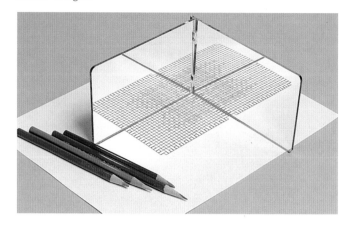

*Hold two small mirrors at right angles to your diagram to see it multiplied.*

Pin the page on a wall for another perspective. If the diagram matches your expectations at this point, continue coloring. If not, change colors on a new weaving diagram and repeat the process.

# Using a Viewfinder

This trick comes from Lois Ericson, author of many books on creative clothing techniques. To preview a weaving design on your chosen garment, draw or photocopy the outline of your garment on a piece of white paper or lightweight card stock. Cut out the shape and then place the "window" over the weaving design.

Outline of Vest

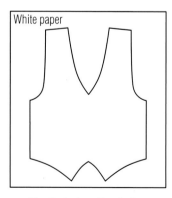

Viewfinder from Vest Outline

You can easily use this method with a weaving diagram and graph paper. For an accurate preview, enlarge or reduce your garment outline on graph paper to correspond with the scale of the weaving pattern. For example, if the back of a vest measures 23" across and you intend to weave with 1"-wide warp strips, count 23 rows across the weaving diagram and match the width of the vest outline to that measurement. Repeat the calculations with the length of the vest and the warp strip measurements. Cut the shape from the graph paper and you'll see that the hole in the viewfinder is in the correct proportion to judge the effect of the woven pattern on the back of your vest.

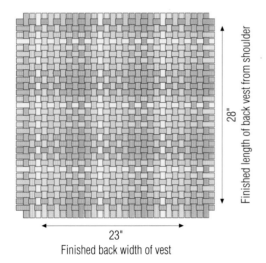

Preview of Vest Back

Finished length of back vest from shoulder 28"

Finished back width of vest 23"

See pages 85–86 in the Appendix for sample viewfinder shapes you can use as you plan your garments.

# PREPARING TO WEAVE

In the woven and quilted process, you assemble the layers, known as the quilt sandwich, as you would for a traditional quilt—top, batting, and backing—but with a twist. Instead of completing the pieced or appliquéd top and then selecting batting and backing, you lay out the batting and backing and weave your strips together on top of them.

For clothing, measure the individual pattern pieces and cut a generous rectangle of backing and batting for each piece to

allow for take-up during quilting. After weaving and quilting, you will place the pattern piece on the woven rectangle and cut the fabric to the correct shape.

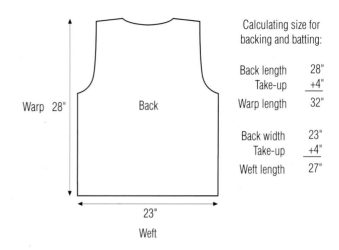

Warp 28"

Back

23"

Weft

Calculating size for backing and batting:

| | |
|---|---|
| Back length | 28" |
| Take-up | +4" |
| Warp length | 32" |
| | |
| Back width | 23" |
| Take-up | +4" |
| Weft length | 27" |

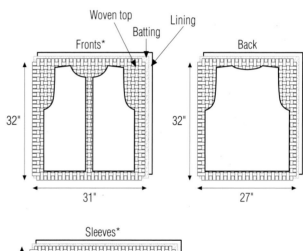

Woven top
Batting
Lining

Fronts*
32"
31"

Back
32"
27"

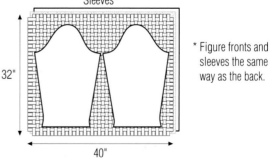

Sleeves*
32"
40"

* Figure fronts and sleeves the same way as the back.

## Backing

Choose a lightweight, yet sturdy fabric for the reverse side of your garment. Many quilters use unbleached muslin for the backing on their quilts, but for garments you need a lighter-weight, more pliable fabric. China silk or a polyester imitation silk is the best choice. These fabrics are strong enough to support a quilted top and smooth enough to slide over other clothing if necessary. Select a color to complement your weaving fabrics. If you prefer and do not mind the additional weight, you can use a lightweight printed cotton for the backing.

Because the pattern layout will be different, you will need more than the yardage requirements given on the pattern for your garment. Purchase enough lining to allow a wide margin around each pattern piece.

## Batting

Batting is the puffy layer between the woven top and the backing. When the three layers of a quilt sandwich (top, batting, and backing) are quilted, the areas between the quilting stitches stand out in relief, adding visual texture and interest.

Many types of batting are available today. Most batting is made of cotton or polyester, or a blend of the two. The choice of fiber content is purely personal.

Batting thickness varies from ⅛" to almost 2". Because the woven quilt top has two layers of fabric, it's important to minimize the bulk and weight for clothing. Choose a smooth, lightweight batting. I prefer Thermore® by Hobbs. Even low-loft batting is too puffy for the woven and quilted clothing shown in this book. If low-loft batting is the only lightweight batting available to you, split it into two layers and use only one. Cotton or polyester batting doesn't need to be prewashed.

You can substitute prewashed cotton flannel for batting, or you can eliminate the batting entirely and weave on top of the backing instead to eliminate as much bulk as possible.

## Fabric Preparation

If your fabrics are washable, you can wash your woven and quilted clothing just as you would traditional pieced and appliquéd wearables. If you tear your fabric strips and remove the raveled threads at the edges, the edges will remain stable, although they will soften slightly with washing. If you cut the strips, some raveling will occur with washing, but it's not usually a problem. To see how the strips of your selected fabrics will look after washing, make a small (12" x 12") woven and quilted sample in your chosen fabrics and wash it.

Of course, you can always dry-clean your wearables if washing seems risky, particularly with tailored jackets and coats or fabrics that should be dry-cleaned.

If you plan to wash your woven and quilted garment, prepare cottons, silks, and other washable fabrics by prewashing to remove the sizing. Wash the fabrics in the washing machine or soak them in a basin of warm water. When prewashing dark fabrics, check the rinse water for traces of dye. If you see dye in the rinse water, continue to rinse until the water is clear. If any fabric keeps running after several washings, it's best to eliminate it from your collection.

If you intend to dry-clean the finished garment, lay a damp press cloth on top of each fabric and lightly press with a steam iron to shrink the yardage and remove any wrinkles.

# PREPARING THE STRIPS

In traditional piecing, the raw edges are hidden by the seams; in traditional appliqué, the raw edges are turned under and stitched in place. Both techniques result in a quilt top that is sturdy and has a neat, flat appearance.

In the woven and quilted process, the strips are not sewn together, which means that the strip edges are exposed. You may leave these edges unfinished or finish them in a variety of ways before you begin to weave. The decision depends on the types of fabrics you use, the look you prefer, and how much time you want to spend getting that look.

Each edge option has advantages, so experiment with your fabrics before beginning a garment.

## Strips with Unfinished Edges

Choose this method if you like the look of raw edges in the weaving. You may tear or cut strips for weaving.

Tearing your fabric into strips is fast and easy—and a great stress reliever! Most cottons, cotton blends, and light- and medium-weight silks tear easily across the fabric from selvage to selvage. You'll need to remove any threads that extend along the torn edges after tearing the strips, but once you press the strips, the edges should not continue to ravel.

Torn edges add a somewhat casual touch and keep your clothing from being too serious. I find that unfinished edges are a great conversation starter, especially with silk or silklike fabrics. Although we've seen lots of washed and sueded silk in recent years, there is still a mystique surrounding this luxurious fabric. I love the surprising combination of casual torn edges on an elegant fabric—not ragged or scruffy edges, just an unexpected soft fringe.

Some prints, especially cottons with black or dark backgrounds, may reveal small dots of white at the edges when they're torn. These specks occur because tearing pulls the warp threads just enough to move them out of alignment in the original weaving pattern. With some fabrics, tearing noticeably changes the color at the edges; with other fabrics, it doesn't. This possibility is another reason to tear a few test strips before beginning a garment. If you like the results, go ahead and use the strips for your garment. If not, choose another finishing method for the edges or choose another, more suitable fabric and try again. Refer to "Tearing Strips" on page 23.

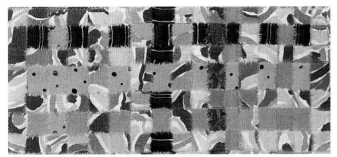
Woven sample with torn strips

Cutting strips is necessary with some fabrics. This is particularly true for specialty fabrics such as lamé and tricot as well as all other knits. If you are using a printed stripe or plaid fabric or one with small printed designs arranged in vertical or horizontal rows, you may want to cut strips following the "line" rather than tear them. Often this type of design is not printed on the straight grain. If straight design lines are important to you, cutting is a must.

Strips that are cut will ravel because you inevitably cut across threads. Don't remove the raveled threads. If you do, the edges of the strips will look uneven. The raveling is not usually objectionable; if occasional threads along the edge don't fit your design concept, try one of the finishing methods described below. See "Rotary Cutting Strips" on page 23.

Cut strips will ravel, as you can see in this close-up of "Blue Checks Out," shown in its entirety on page 62.

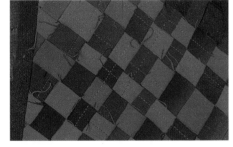

Cutting some or all of the strips gives you a great deal of flexibility in how you can use a printed fabric. To add a strong directional element to your woven piece, try cutting strips with curved edges.

Woven sample with random-cut strips

Another way to bring movement to a design is to cut striped fabric on the diagonal. Just remember that the bias edges will stretch easily and must be handled with care.

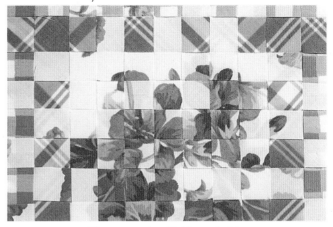
Woven sample with bias-cut strips

Precut strips of fabric available on rolls are an alternative to cutting or tearing the strips yourself. Weavers often use fabric strips as weft when they're making rugs. Check with a shop that sells yarn or weaving supplies to see if it carries rolls of fabric strips, similar to rolls of ribbon. One example of this "yarn" is Poppanna from Finland. It's actually a ⅜"-wide bias strip of cotton fabric that comes in many wonderful colors. See "Resources" on page 87.

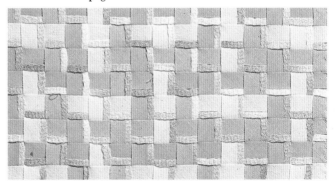
Woven sample using Poppanna and flat cotton yarn

## Strips with Finished Edges

If you decide to finish the edges of your strips, you have two options. You may finish the raw edges by machine or you may turn under the raw edges. Some sewing machines have decorative or utility stitches that you can use to finish the edges. A simple zigzag stitch may be all you want, but you can also experiment with other stitches. Test the stitch width, length, and tension on your fabric.

Serging is one of the neatest and quickest ways to machine finish cut edges and offers you the opportunity to add another dimension to your weaving. You can serge the edges using matching thread, or you can choose a decorative thread in a matching or contrasting color for added interest. For highlights, consider using metallic or rayon thread in a shade darker or lighter than the fabric. You may want to try different colors of thread on adjacent strips or use a variegated thread. Try simple serging or a rolled-edge finish. Consult one of the many available books on serging for information on how to work with decorative threads. See the bibliography on page 87. The "Mother-of-the-Bride Cocoon" jacket (page 60) has strips with serged edges.

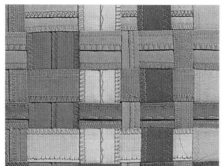

*Woven sample
with serged edges*

Folding under the cut edges gives your woven piece a quiet, elegant look. Cut each strip twice the finished width plus ¼" and fold the cut edges lengthwise to overlap ¼" at the center back. Press the strip flat, turn it over, and weave with the smooth side up.

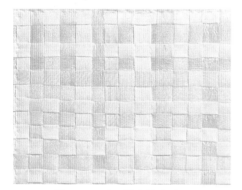

*Woven sample with folded edges*

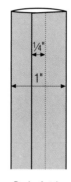

Back of strip

To create a different look, cut and fold the strips so that a hint of the wrong side shows. This variation is very effective with a fabric whose wrong side is just as appealing as its right side, or a fabric whose wrong side contrasts sharply with its right side. For 1"-wide finished strips, cut the strips 1¾" wide, then turn under ⅜" along each long edge, revealing a ¼"-wide "stripe" of the wrong side of the fabric. Use this side of the prepared strip as the right side when you begin to weave.

Since, in effect, you're adding another layer to the quilted top of your garment when you fold the edges of the strips, consider the weight of the fabric before you choose this method.

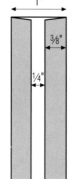

Back of strip
becomes right side
in woven piece.

Fabric tubes are another variation on folded-edge strips.

1. Cut each strip twice the desired finished width plus ½".
2. *With right sides together,* stitch ¼" from the long edges.
3. With the tip of your iron, press the seam open.
4. Turn the tube right side out and press it with the seam centered on the back.

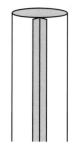

Back of strip
with right sides
together

Another option is to stitch a tube and leave it unturned. Because a fabric tube adds an additional layer to the quilted top, it is best to use very lightweight fabrics for this method. You can start with the right or the wrong sides together, depending on the colors in the fabric and the effect you want. Press the seam open.

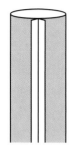

Back of strip
with wrong sides
together

Decorative ribbons, with their finished edges, are also easy to use for woven and quilted projects. Ribbon and rickrack were used to create the beautiful fabric for the blouse shown on page 61. Ribbons are sometimes very tightly woven and can be difficult to quilt by hand. They're also more expensive than fabric, but you'll find many exquisite ribbons in fabric stores, and they make a nice accent when mixed with fabric strips.

Lace adds a delicate touch to woven and quilted clothing. If the lace is fairly heavy and densely woven, you can weave it as you would a fabric strip. If it's narrow, lightweight, or has uneven edges, lay the lace on top of a fabric strip; anchor with a dot of glue every inch or so. Treat this double strip as one when you weave.

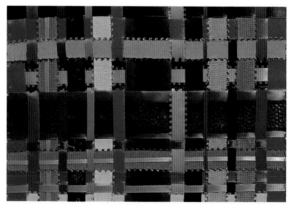

*Woven sample with lace and ribbons*

# TEARING STRIPS

Most of the garments in this book were made with warp and weft fabric strips that were torn along the crosswise grain. To tear fabric strips, follow these steps:

1. Determine the warp and weft strip width and length. In woven and quilted garments, strips are usually ¾" to 1½" wide. It's possible to tear ½"- or even ¼"-wide strips if the fabric is very closely woven. Test first.

   The strips will vary in length according to the length and width of the individual pattern pieces. For example, the warp strips for the back of a vest may be 28" long, while those for the back of a coat may be 54" long or longer. Refer to page 19 for calculations.

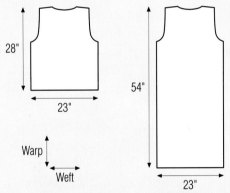

The length of the weft strips is determined by the width of the garment piece at its widest point plus a few inches for take-up during quilting. For strips that are longer than the width of the fabric you are using, prepare two strips and join them with fusible web as explained in "Changing Strips in Mid-row," page 26.

2. Begin with a straight edge. Before you begin to tear strips, clip the selvage at one end of the fabric and tear across to the other selvage to create a straight edge.

3. Mark the strips. Measure and mark the fabric lightly along one selvage in increments equal to the desired strip width. Mark as many warp and weft strips as you need from each fabric.

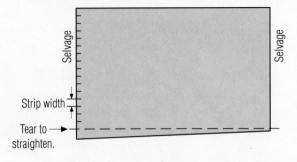

4. Snip the fabric at the marks and tear each strip to the length you need or all the way across the fabric width. The edges will curl and ravel. Trim away the raveled threads and press each strip.

# ROTARY CUTTING STRIPS

You may choose to cut rather than tear your warp and weft strips. Because strips for weaving must be perfectly straight, it's better to cut a single layer of fabric rather than fold the fabric as you would for other rotary cutting. Follow these simple steps to cut the strips:

1. Press the fabric and lay it flat on the cutting mat.
2. For strips cut on the cross grain, align your square ruler with the selvage; place your cutting ruler to the left.
3. Remove the square and cut along the edge of the ruler, rolling the cutter away from you.
4. Move the ruler to the right, aligning the ruler markings at the desired strip width with the cut edge of the fabric. Cut the fabric into strips, moving your ruler as necessary if the strips are long.

5. To cut strips on the lengthwise grain, trim one selvage. Cut strips parallel to the selvage.

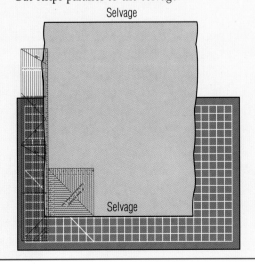

# CREATING THE WOVEN YARDAGE

Now it's time to put all the pieces together to create woven and quilted yardage. After you read through the weaving and quilting directions that follow, I suggest that you refer to them often as you make a simple vest using the pattern for "Summer Dreamin'" that is included at the back of this book. Complete directions begin on page 38.

Making a simple project first is a good way to acquaint yourself with the sequence, master the weaving process, and experiment with color.

## Preparing the Pattern

1. Select the fabrics, the garment pattern, and the weaving pattern, not necessarily in that order. You may have only a general idea of what the final garment will look like. Or you may have already colored a weaving diagram to match your fabric choices and cut a viewfinder in the garment shape for a more visible plan. Either way, remain flexible as you work through the weaving and quilting because new ideas can occur at any point in the process.

   If you are using one of the garment patterns provided at the back of this book, trace the pieces in the appropriate size onto tracing paper or pattern tracing cloth.

2. Make a muslin to check the fit of the pattern. (See "Checking the Fit—Making a Muslin" on page 14.) As mentioned previously, a test sample is very important to the success of your garment. Attention to fitting details now will let you concentrate on the fun of weaving and quilting with no nagging worries about the fit of your completed garment.

3. Transfer the final alterations from the muslin to the paper pattern for a permanent reference.

   NOTE: Sometimes the muslin has several slashes and tucks that may be confusing, so the paper pattern with the final changes is a valuable resource. If you want to cut a flat piece of fabric, the pattern piece must also lie flat. Be sure to taper the edges of any tucks or slashes across the pattern until it lies flat.

4. If you are using a pattern that has standard facings and a hem, but you plan to finish the edges with binding, cut away all but ⅝" of the hem allowance now. Do not remove the seam allowances around the neckline and along the front edges. When you are ready to bind these edges, stitch

¾" from the raw edges, then trim away the ⅝"-wide seam allowance, leaving ⅛" extending beyond the stitching. The stitching will be covered by the binding.

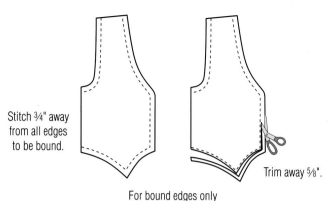

Stitch ¾" away from all edges to be bound.

Trim away ⅝".

For bound edges only

## Weaving

1. Use the individual pattern pieces to determine the dimensions of the backing and batting for each piece. Be sure to measure the paper pattern at its longest and widest points and add 4" to each measurement. This will give you the dimensions for the working size, which allows for take-up during quilting. Four inches is the minimum take-up allowance. If you are weaving yardage for an exceptionally wide pattern piece, as for "Summer Dreamin'" (page 38), it's a good idea to add even more for take-up allowance. A little extra width or length in the finished weaving allows you some leeway in placing the pattern pieces for the best use of any design you have created in the woven piece.

2. Cut the backing and batting for each garment piece. Select one piece to weave and set the others aside. When

### HOW TO WEAVE IDENTICAL FRONTS

To weave two separate fronts identically, make a duplicate paper pattern of the front. Lay the pattern pieces side by side with the center fronts almost touching. Cut one large rectangle of backing and batting with a 4" margin all around the perimeter. You will weave enough for both fronts and cut them apart after quilting.

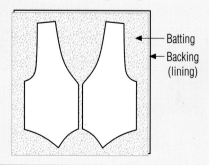

Batting

Backing (lining)

making a vest or jacket with several pieces, I often start with the back because it's the largest uninterrupted surface. Of course, if you are weaving identical fronts using the method shown in the box on page 24, it will be approximately the same size as the piece for the back.

3. Pin or tape the backing, right side down, to your work surface. Place the batting on top of the backing and anchor it in place.

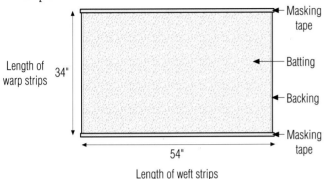

4. Tear or cut and press the number of warp strips for each pattern piece according to the weaving diagram you'll be using. Measure the backing from the top edge to the bottom to determine the length of the strips for the warp.

The width of the strips is a personal choice. Many of the garments in this book were made with 1"-wide strips, but choose the width that works best for your garment and weaving pattern. You might decide to use various widths in a random sequence or follow a structured pattern. (See "Preparing the Strips" on page 20.) Keep in mind that wider strips make the finished piece appear wider than a

piece woven with narrower strips. If you wish to use narrow strips, do a tear test. It may be difficult to tear strips narrower than ¾". However, you can rotary cut narrower strips. (See "Rotary Cutting Strips" on page 23.)

5. Lay the vertical warp strips, right side up, in sequence across the batting. To keep the warp straight and provide the right amount of tension, use pins or tape to secure the strips at the upper and lower edges. Check to make sure that all the warp strips are snug against each other but not overlapping.

6. Measure the width of the backing to determine the length of the weft strips. Tear or cut and press the weft strips as you did the warp. For a very wide piece, such as "Summer Dreamin,'" you may need to piece the weft strips for the proper length. (See "Changing Strips in Mid-row," page 26.)

The weft strips may also be of any width you choose. You can use strips of the same width throughout, or you can vary the widths.

Manipulating the weft strips to highlight a certain color or part of a print is an easy way to add design details to your woven and quilted clothing. The Bargello effect in the weaving pattern for "Summer Dreamin'" was created by moving the color bars of the weft strips in sequence, first to the right and then to the left. (Bargello is an Italian word used to describe a flame-stitch pattern in canvas work.)

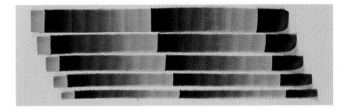

*Adjust the weft strip placement to create a Bargello pattern in the finished piece.*

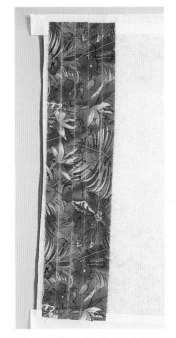

*Arrange the vertical warp strips in the desired sequence.*

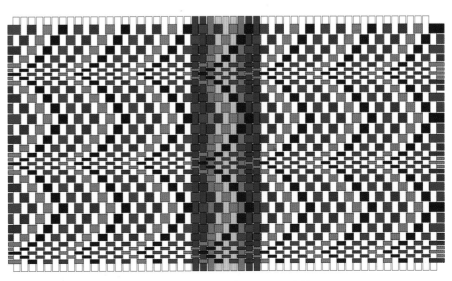

Weaving diagram for "Summer Dreamin'"

7. Begin weaving the weft strips in and out of the warp strips. Referring to your weaving pattern, pick up a weft strip and slide it over and under the warp yarns as needed to imitate the first row of the pattern. When you reach the opposite edge, hold the ends in your fingers at each end and pull the strip taut to make it lie straight and flat.

   Lay your rotary ruler on top of the strip and adjust any areas that are not straight. Pin each end of the strip to the batting and backing.

   Weave the second weft strip, following the pattern for row 2 in the weaving diagram.

8. Continue weaving the remaining weft strips in sequence, smoothing and straightening the warp strips as you go. After every other weft strip, use your rotary ruler to make sure the warp and weft are straight and perpendicular to each other.

   If you're not comfortable weaving with your fingers, use a weaving or craft needle. You can also make your own needle. (See "Weaving & Sewing Tools" on page 16.)

*A weaving needle guides the weft strip over and under the warp.*

## Marking and Basting the Layers

After the weaving is finished, you must anchor the strips to keep them from shifting while you quilt.

1. Decide on the quilting pattern you want to use and mark it lightly on the woven yardage if necessary.
2. Pin-baste to hold the layers together securely while you stitch. Careful pin basting helps prevent distortion and eliminates unwanted tucks or puckers in the backing. Use straight pins to pin-baste for hand quilting; for machine quilting, use small safety pins. Position them so that you can easily remove them while you are stitching if necessary. I usually pin every intersection where the fabric strips cross each other. It takes a lot of pins, but it makes the quilting so much easier.

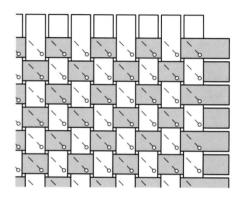

---

## CHANGING STRIPS IN MID-ROW

Changing fabrics in mid-row gives you much more flexibility, allowing you to alter the pattern or color of your design. Sometimes it's effective to see only a small area of color in a row of weaving, rather than an entire warp or weft strip of the fabric. As you weave, you can easily attach a strip of one fabric to another and hide the join under a cross strip. The change can be made in a warp or weft row.

1. To join a strip of fabric B to a strip of fabric A, cut the ends of the strips so that they will overlap under the nearest cross strip.
2. Apply a ½" square of paper-backed fusible web to the end of strip A on the right side. Peel off the paper and place strip B on top of strip A. Fuse the ends together, following the manufacturer's instructions, and continue weaving.

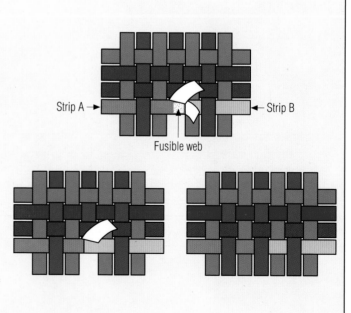

Strip A →  ← Strip B

Fusible web

---

# QUILTING WOVEN YARDAGE

With your woven piece well basted, you're ready to quilt by hand or machine. There are many options for quilting designs. Follow the warp and weft strips with straight stitching for a simple grid, or stitch diagonal lines across the intersections in crosshatch or zigzag patterns. You can superimpose a free-form or traditional pattern on top of the weaving by tracing the pattern onto a piece of water-soluble stabilizer, pinning it to the woven top, and stitching along the traced lines.

Consider the quilting thread as carefully as you choose the fabrics. A change of thread color keeps the eye moving across the surface to enliven your quilting design. You might incorporate shiny rayons or glittery metallics to highlight the focal point of your garment.

NOTE: If you prefer not to quilt, you can tie the layers together with yarn or floss. Sewing beads or buttons at the intersections of warp and weft adds a whimsical touch of embellishment.

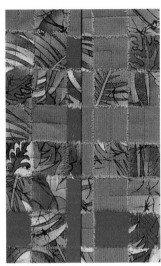

*Random lines of quilting result in a yardage with a soft hand.*

*Every intersection has been stitched once in a zigzag pattern.*

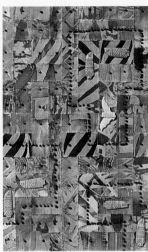

*Beads and buttons hold the layers together in these two playful pieces.*

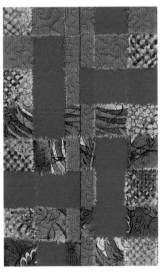

*Every intersection has been stitched twice, adding a little more firmness to the finished piece.*

*Stipple quilting results in a firm hand, with every strip intersection heavily stitched.*

Think about how much quilting you wish to do, remembering that heavy quilting adds to the weight and the stiffness of the fabric. For example, while allover stipple quilting is lovely on quilts, it would add substantially to the weight of a garment. Better to use it in small doses for emphasis.

In addition to choosing the design and the thread, you must also decide whether you wish to quilt by hand or machine.

## Hand Quilting

Hand quilting adds a delicate and often nostalgic look to your woven and quilted garment. Because there is one more layer of fabric than usual where the fabric strips cross each other, you may need to adjust your needle size for more comfortable stitching. You can put a piece of woven yardage on your floor frame and quilt as usual, or use a hand-held hoop for smaller pieces. Take extra care in putting the fabric into your hoop to avoid distorting the strip alignment.

## Machine Quilting

Machine quilting is ideal for woven yardage because it's easy to stitch through the two layers of fabric. If you've hesitated to machine quilt in the past, a woven piece is an ideal first project. Before you begin, make sure your machine is in good working order. Replace the needle with a fresh one to avoid damaging your fabric.

For a simple grid pattern, begin at the right edge of the woven yardage and quilt the warp rows first; then turn the piece and quilt the weft rows. Note that instead of starting to stitch in the center of the piece and working outward as you would when machine quilting a more traditional quilt top, it is best to begin at the right-hand edge with woven yardage. As you work toward the center, remove the pins and roll the piece into a cylinder to keep it out of the way.

If your quilting lines start or stop in the interior of the piece, you'll need to clean-finish the beginning and ending points. Pull the top thread through to the back, tie the top and bobbin threads together in a small knot, and thread them through a hand sewing needle with a large eye. Run the needle under the backing into the batting for an inch. Bring the needle up and clip the excess thread.

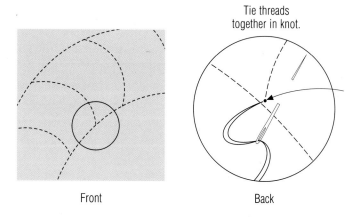

Front          Back

Clean-Finish Quilting Lines

## MACHINE-QUILTING TIPS

The following machine-quilting tips will make your work faster and more enjoyable:

- Make sure your machine is clean and well oiled. If it's been a while since your machine was professionally cleaned and tuned, this is the time to do it. Lint in the gears or poorly adjusted tension discs will take away the fun of working on your quilt.
- Use the proper needle. (See "Weaving & Sewing Tools" on page 16 for help in choosing the right machine-quilting needle.) Because it's difficult to see the small nicks that can cause the thread to fray, start with a new needle at the beginning of each project. At the hint of a problem with the needle, replace it to avoid unsightly snags and pulls in your fabric. This is especially important when working with lightweight and delicate dressmaking fabrics.
- Use good-quality thread. Inexpensive thread breaks more easily, especially when going through several layers. The frustration is not worth the savings.
- Loosen the tension slightly. If your machine has a dial for the pressure setting, loosen it too. Often the darning setting is best for machine quilting.
- Use a walking foot. This special presser foot is designed to guide all the layers in a quilt sandwich under the needle at the same time. If you're not familiar with a walking foot, ask your sewing-machine dealer for a demonstration. You'll be amazed at how evenly you can stitch with the proper presser foot. If your machine has a built-in even-feed feature, you won't need a walking foot.
- If you are using a regular presser foot instead of a walking foot, try this trick to prevent the top layer of fabric from scooting in front of the foot, causing unsightly wrinkles and tucks:
  1. Sew for a few inches, then stop.
  2. Raise the presser foot and smooth the fabric as needed. Stopping and raising the presser foot periodically releases some of the pressure on the top layer so that all three layers feed evenly and smoothly along the length of the seam.
  3. Lower the presser foot and sew for a few more inches, then stop. Raise the presser foot and repeat the process, smoothing the fabric and sewing a few inches at a time.
- Run the machine at a consistent, comfortable speed that feeds the fabric under the needle evenly.
- For detailed machine-quilting instructions, refer to the books listed in the bibliography on page 87.

# FREE-MOTION MACHINE QUILTING

You can quilt part or all of your woven top with an unstructured design. You may enjoy stitching free-form swirls and waves or you may like the security of tracing a drawn line. Using water-soluble stabilizer on top of the weaving gives you a smooth surface for stitching, along with the option of a predrawn design.

Bamboo leaves from an Asian print inspired the machine embroidery on the back of this vest.

*Gold metallic thread highlights the bamboo leaves in this Asian print-inspired design.*

You can duplicate this idea with your own fabric:
1. Select the part of the design you want to highlight. Take your fabric to a copy machine, lay it smoothly on the glass, and make a copy.

*The copy made from the printed fabric.*

2. Use this copy to begin your design. You may want to enlarge the original or cut it up and rearrange parts of it to fit the size and shape of your pattern piece. Make as many changes as you need to simplify the shapes.

Cover your final design with a piece of water-soluble stabilizer and trace the design lines with a paint pen in a color that contrasts with the woven yardage.

*Trace the shapes with a paint pen that contrasts with your fabric.*

3. Place the tracing on top of your woven yardage. Check the position by laying the pattern piece over the tracing. Remove any basting pins that are under the tracing. Pin the stabilizer to your woven fabric and stitch over the traced lines.
4. Following the manufacturer's instructions, dissolve the stabilizer in water, blot, and allow to dry flat. When it is completely dry, continue with the rest of the quilting as desired.

## CHAPTER 4

# Garment Cutting, Assembly & Finishing

When you have completed your weaving and have quilted the layers together, you are ready to cut and assemble the pieces. You will need to decide how you will finish the seams and the raw edges. Before you cut the garment, read this chapter so you know your options. Those included here are the basics; you may come up with some innovative ideas of your own.

## CUTTING & ASSEMBLING THE PIECES

1. After completing the desired quilting, lightly press your woven and quilted yardage and position the paper pattern on top of it. If you plan to bind the edges of the garment, position the pattern piece so that the bottom edge lies along the bottom edge of one of the weft strips if possible. If there is a ⅝" seam allowance at the bottom edge, *place the cutting line* along the bottom edge of a strip.

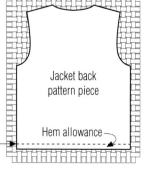

For bound edges, place bottom edge of pattern at bottom edge of a weft strip.

Right front pattern piece | Left front pattern piece

If you plan to hem the garment, place the hem fold line in the center of a strip. Pin in place and cut out the pieces.

Jacket back pattern piece

Hemline in center of strip

Hem allowance

2. Staystitch ½" from all cut edges to hold the strip ends in place, out of the way of construction stitching.
3. Assemble the garment, following the pattern instructions and using the seam and edge finishes of your choice.

## FINISHING THE SEAMS

Since the backing often (but not always) acts as the lining in woven and quilted garments, you will want to neatly finish the seam edges inside the garment. I have found a flat-felled seam to be the most inconspicuous and effective seam finish for the majority of the garments I make. It is appropriate for any straight or gently curved seam. Other alternatives include mock flat-felled seams and bound seams and hem edges. Serging is appropriate too. Consider using a decorative or contrasting thread in the upper looper to add a decorative touch on the inside of your garment.

Flat-felled seam

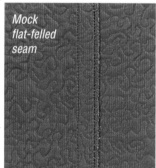

Mock flat-felled seam

Plain seam with bound edges

Plain seam with serged edges

For some garment styles—for example, a bomber jacket like the one shown in the photo on page 55—you will probably want to make a traditional lining from a slippery fabric. In that case, the extra lining will be attached in the conventional manner, covering the unfinished seam edges, so it is not necessary to do a special seam finish. Simply stitch and press the seams open as you normally would.

## Flat-Felled Seams

When you are making a traditional flat-felled seam, the garment pieces are placed wrong sides together. For woven and quilted garments, this is not desirable. Instead, *stitch all seams with right sides together as usual.*

1. Stitch each seam, using a ⅝"-wide seam allowance (or the width specified for the pattern you are using).
2. Press the seam open, then press again along the seam line on the woven side to make sure there are no tucks or wrinkles.
3. On the inside of the garment, trim the front seam allowance so it is ⅛" to ¼" wide.

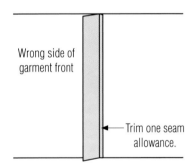

Wrong side of garment front

Trim one seam allowance.

4. Turn the back seam allowance over the narrower front allowance and press. Then turn under and press an even ¼" along the raw edge of the remaining seam allowance.
5. Hand slipstitch the folded edge to the backing fabric on the inside of the garment.

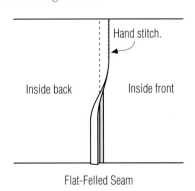

Hand stitch.

Inside back    Inside front

Flat-Felled Seam

## Mock Flat-Felled Seams

This seam is quick and easy but will be more conspicuous on the inside of the garment. Machine stitching to hold the seam edges in place will show on the right side of the garment, so select a thread color for the bobbin that blends with the woven and quilted fabric.

1. Stitch the seam and press open. Press on the right side.
2. Trim one seam allowance to ¼". If desired, pink or serge the long raw edge of the remaining seam allowance, then turn it over the narrower one and press.

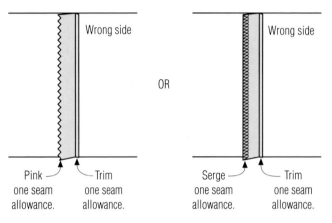

Wrong side    Wrong side

OR

Pink one seam allowance.    Trim one seam allowance.    Serge one seam allowance.    Trim one seam allowance.

3. Stitch ¼" to ⅜" from the seam line through all layers.

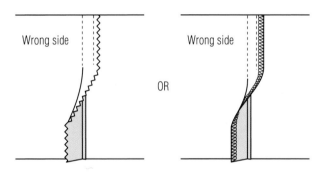

Wrong side    Wrong side

OR

## Bound Seams

If you prefer plain seams that are stitched, then pressed open on the inside of the garment, you can bind them to cover the raw edges and add a custom-finished look to the inside of the garment.

1. Stitch the seams and press them open.
2. Choose a lightweight fabric, such as China silk or silk organza, for the binding in a matching or contrasting color. Cut 1½"-wide strips from the chosen fabric. If you will be binding a curved edge, cut the strips on the bias.
3. With right sides together and raw edges even, stitch a bias strip to each seam allowance. Use a ¼"-wide seam. (Use

the outer edge of the ¼" quilting presser foot if available for your machine.)

4. Turn the bias over the seam edge to the underside of the seam allowance and press. Stitch in-the-ditch from the right side of the seam allowance to catch the underlayer of the bias. Trim close to the stitching on the underside of the seam allowance.

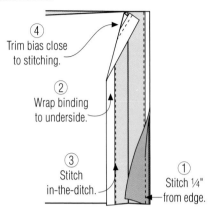

④ Trim bias close to stitching.

② Wrap binding to underside.

③ Stitch in-the-ditch.

① Stitch ¼" from edge.

**NOTE:** If your garment will have a traditional hem, use the binding method described above to finish the raw edge before hemming.

## Serged Seams

If you have a serger, use it to do a fast and neat finish on the edges of traditional seams. Experiment with the stitch width and length on scraps of your woven and quilted yardage, then serge each edge. Use a contrasting thread in the upper looper to lend a designer touch.

*Decorative thread in the upper looper of a serger, set for a closely spaced stitch, adds a designer touch to simple seams.*

# FINISHING THE EDGES

Since you don't need to attach a separate lining or facings to most woven and quilted garments, consider binding the outer edges with bias binding cut from one or more of the weaving fabrics. To finish the edge of her jacket, "Jewels in Motion"

(page 58), Bonnie Berlin cleverly pieced together strips of several fabrics used in the jacket.

Of course, you can face and line a woven and quilted garment if you prefer. I lined my bomber jacket, "Purplefest" (page 55), and used facings and a traditional hem on my blazer, "Shadow Waltz"(page 56). Notice the trim used to cover the raw edges of the hem on the inside of this jacket.

*Traditional lining in a bomber-style jacket*

*Traditional facing and hem in a more tailored style*

Consider other unique and unconventional finishing methods as well. For example, Bonnie Berlin's vest, "Color Rhythms" (page 51), has a raw-edge finish on the armholes, around the neckline, and down the front. At the bottom edge, she tied pairs of adjoining warp strips in a knot. A double row of zigzag stitching in metallic thread holds the layers together at the outer edges.

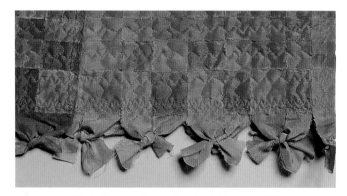

*Playful knots and raw edges finish Bonnie Berlin's "Color Rhythms" vest, shown in full on page 51.*

# Binding

For clothing, I use a single-layer binding rather than the double-fold binding found on most quilts, because it's less bulky.

To determine how wide to cut single-layer binding strips, decide on the desired finished width, multiply by 4, and add ½" for the turn of the folds plus slight stretching due to the bias cut. For example, for a ⅜"-wide finished binding, you would cut 2"-wide strips. Cut the binding on the true bias so it will fold smoothly around curved edges. To determine the total amount of bias needed, measure the cut edges and add 5" for overlap.

If you need a long piece of binding—for example, to bind the outer edge of a long jacket—cut the ends of the binding pieces at a 45° angle and sew them together as shown. Press the seams open to eliminate lumps in the finished binding.

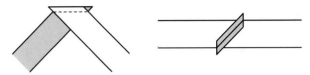

If the pattern you are using was designed specifically for bound edges, follow the steps below to apply the binding. *However, if you are using a pattern originally designed and cut for a garment finished with traditional facings, you will need to remove the seam allowances from the edges you are binding.* To do this, stitch ⅛" inside the given seam line. For example, if your pattern has ⅝"-wide seam allowances, stitch ¾" from all raw edges that you are binding. Then trim away the seam allowance, leaving ⅛" of fabric extending beyond the stitching. The stitching will be covered by the binding.

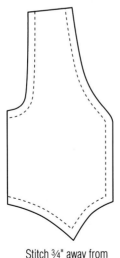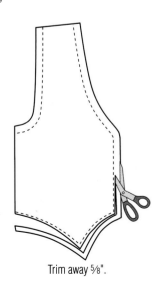

Stitch ¾" away from all edges to be bound.

Trim away ⅝".

1. At one end of the bias binding strip, turn under and press ¼" at a 45° angle.

2. Beginning at a side seam at the lower edge of the garment, align the raw edge of the strip with the raw edge of the garment. Pin the binding to the garment. Stitch the desired distance from the raw edge; for example, if you want binding that finishes to ⅜", use a ⅜"-wide seam allowance.

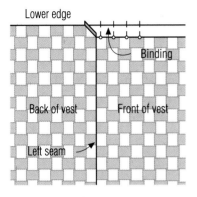

Lower edge

Binding

Back of vest

Front of vest

Left seam

3. If the garment has square corners at the bottom edge, miter the corners as shown on page 34.

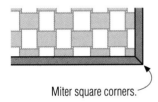

Miter square corners.

4. Continue pinning and stitching the binding to the garment edge until you reach the starting point. Lap the binding over the folded end of the strip for about 2"; trim away the excess bias strip. Complete the stitching and backstitch to secure.

5. Turn the bias to the inside of the garment, turning under the remaining raw edge so that it just barely covers the stitching. Press carefully and pin the binding in place, distributing fullness evenly around the curved edges. Slipstitch in place.

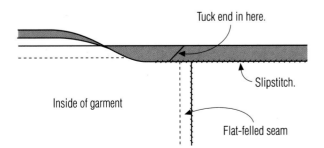

Tuck end in here.

Slipstitch.

Inside of garment

Flat-felled seam

# MITERED-CORNER BINDING APPLICATION

1. Complete step 1 of "Binding" on page 33.
2. With raw edges aligned, pin and stitch the binding to the edge of the garment, beginning at a side seam for an inconspicuous join. Use a seam allowance that matches the desired finished width of the binding. When you reach the first corner, stop stitching a seam-allowance's width away. If you want a ⅜"-wide finished binding, stop stitching ⅜" from the corner, pivot, and stitch to the corner at a 45° angle. Clip the threads.

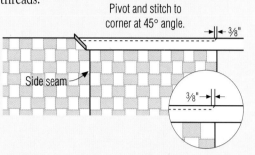

3. Fold binding straight up and away from the garment to form a 45° angle at the stitched corner. Finger-press the fold.

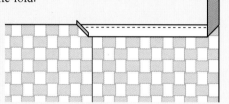

4. Hold the diagonal fold in place with your finger while you bring the binding straight down. (The binding will form a fold even with the upper edge of the garment.) Pin. Beginning at the top of the fold, stitch, using the same seam width as you did for the first side of the corner.

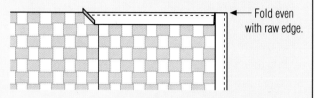

5. Continue pinning and stitching the binding to the garment, mitering the corners as described above.
6. Turn the binding to the inside over the raw edge of the garment, turning under the remaining raw edge of the binding so that it just barely covers the stitching. Miters will form at each corner. Press and pin carefully. Slipstitch in place.

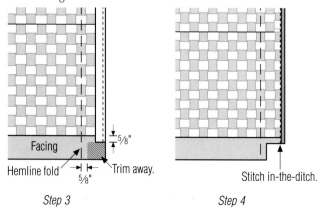

## Hemming

For a more conventional finish, face the front edges of a jacket or coat with plain fabric and turn up conventional hems at the bottom edges.

1. After attaching the facing, try on the garment and turn up the hem allowances. Pin in place. The folded edge of the hem should fall in the center of a weft strip if possible.
2. Remove the garment, press the turned allowances, and trim the hem allowance to an even width all around. Trim the side seam allowances in the hem allowance to ¼" and trim the facing hem allowance to ⅝" as shown in the illustration for step 3 at right.

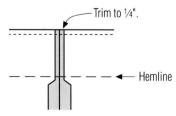

3. Cut a 1"-wide bias strip long enough to finish the hem edge. With right sides together and raw edges even, stitch ¼" from the raw edges.
4. Turn the binding over the raw edge and press. From the right side, stitch in-the-ditch next to the binding. On the wrong side of the hem allowance, trim the bias close to the stitching.

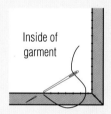

*Step 3*

*Step 4*

5. Turn the hem up, press, and baste in place along the inner edge of the binding.

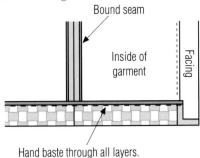

Bound seam

Inside of garment

Facing

Hand baste through all layers.

6. With the bulk of the garment in your lap, turn the hem back along the basting and catchstitch the two layers together along the binding stitching. Remove the basting; press.

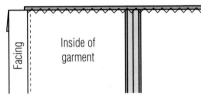

Facing

Inside of garment

7. Turn the front facing to the inside and slipstitch in place along the bottom and inner edges.

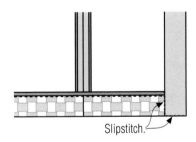

Inside of garment

Slipstitch.

## Lining

If you are making a jacket or vest that will have constructed pockets, such as double welts, you may want to add a separate lining to cover the inner construction, including the seam edges, which will not then require a special finish.

If you plan to make a separate lining, do your weaving on the batting or filler fabric only. Then construct the garment following the pattern guide sheet. In some cases, you will have a facing; in others, the lining will extend to the outer edge of the finished garment.

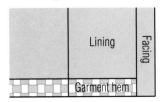

Lining

Facing

Garment hem

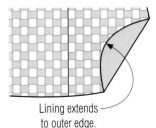

Lining extends to outer edge.

# PROBLEM SOLVING

**Q.** *I have a small piece of woven tapestry that coordinates with my favorite slacks. How can I incorporate it into a woven and quilted vest?*

**A.** The tapestry is probably heavier than the other fabrics you'll use for your vest, but you can use it in small amounts. Woven tapestry ravels badly when cut; plan to zigzag, serge, or encase the raw edges of the weaving strips with a narrow binding. Cut a strip and test the desired edge finish. For weaving, select fabrics that coordinate with the colors in the tapestry. Keep these fabrics in subtle, muted colors and prints to highlight the tapestry fabric. Piece short lengths of the tapestry into the warp or weft randomly or in sequence to form a structured design. (See "Changing Strips in Mid-row" on page 26.)

**Q.** *The fabric I want to use for the yoke of a blouse is the perfect color, but it's flimsy. Can I use it?*

**A.** To add body to a lightweight fabric, back it with a lightweight fusible interfacing. Strips cut from fabric backed in this manner will not ravel. Use a lightweight nonwoven interfacing or try one of the *super-lightweight* fusible knits if available at your fabric store. These interfacings come in white, black, and sometimes tan. Test each to select the one that will not alter the color of the fabric. Cut the strips from the fabric; do not try to tear them.

**Q.** *Help! I didn't allow enough extra fabric for take-up during quilting and now my vest pattern doesn't fit on the woven and quilted piece.*

**A.** This is when your "creativity genes" get a good workout. Don't give up; there are several things you can try. You may find that the new vest is more interesting than your original idea.

- If the section that won't fit is small, such as at the shoulder or back neckline, you can hand sew extra lining and batting to the woven piece and then extend the warp and weft as shown in "Changing Strips in Mid-row" on page 26. It might be necessary to undo a few quilting stitches, then extend the quilting to cover the addition.
- Expand your woven and quilted yardage by cutting it into squares and combining the squares with pieced or appliquéd blocks left from other projects. Use the following procedure:

1. Quilt the pieced and appliquéd blocks with batting and backing to match the woven yardage.

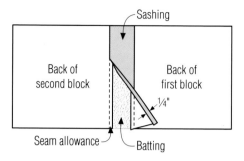

der ¼" on the long edge of the sashing on the back; slipstitch to the backing of the second block.

2. To follow the example above:

   3 strips of sashing for the backing, each 1½" wide and the length of the block

   3 strips of sashing for the right side of the woven and quilted yardage, each 1½" wide and the length of the block

   3 strips of Thermore batting, each 1½" wide and the length of the block

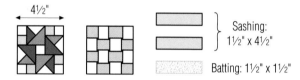

3. At the right edge of 3 of the blocks, layer the pieces as follows: Place the batting strip on the bottom, followed by the back sashing strip, right side up. Then add the quilted block, right side up, and place the front sashing strip on top, right side down. With all raw edges even and using a ¼"-wide seam allowance, stitch the layers together. Trim the batting close to the stitching.

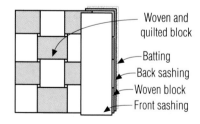

4. Arrange the blocks, alternating the pieced or appliquéd blocks with the woven blocks, to make a row in the required width for your pattern piece.

5. With right sides together, stitch the remaining long edge of the front sashing of one block to the left side of a second block. Trim ¼" from the long unstitched edge of the batting and tuck it under the seam allowances. Turn un-

6. For each completed row of blocks, cut:

   1 strip of sashing for the backing, 1½" wide and the length of the block row

   1 strip of sashing for the front, 1½" wide and the length of the block row

   1 strip of Thermore batting, 1½" wide and the length of the block row

7. Attach the batting and sashing strips to the row of blocks and to the woven and quilted yardage in the manner described in steps 3–5.

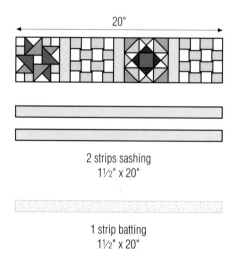

For a Crazy quilt effect, use the method described above, using irregularly shaped pieces.

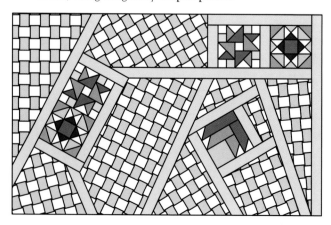

**Q:** *My finished woven and quilted piece is too stiff for the jacket I intended to make. What now?*

**A:** If you've used washable fabrics, fold the pieces, place them inside a pillowcase, and baste it closed. Add the pillowcase to your next load of clothes and let the action of the washing machine soften the fabrics. Take the pieces out of the pillowcase after washing and dry them, one at a time, in a dryer on low heat. Repeat if the yardage is not soft enough after the first wash.

If your fabrics are not washable, use small pieces in detail areas (yoke, pocket, collar, cuffs) or use the yardage to make one-of-a-kind totes or handbags.

**Q:** *How can I add life to my woven and quilted vest? It's boring.*

**A:** Try one of the following ideas:

- Embellish with buttons or beads. You could create a checkerboard yoke effect by sewing buttons in every other square, or outline the edges with a combination of beads and buttons. Barbara Weiland sewed seed beads at the woven intersections and in the center of the strips on her jacket, "Japanese Fantasy Garden" (page 54). This created a yokelike detail on the jacket front. She also outlined the inner edge of the binding with multiple decorative yarns loosely twisted together and couched in place by hand.

*Twisted yarns and beads add sparkle to a simple cardigan style.*

- Add more quilting lines with rayon or metallic threads. Echo the original quilting or create a new design.
- Thread very narrow ribbon through a large-eye needle. Weave into parts of the warp or weft for a color accent.

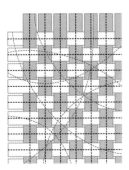

---------- Original quilting

---------- More quilting with metallic threads

---------- Original quilting

========= Narrow ribbon

**Q:** *I've finished weaving with cut strips. They are fraying more than I thought they would, and it spoils the crisp look I intended. Is there any way to fix it?*

**A:** You could cover the raw edges and quilt at the same time. Use a medium-width, closely spaced zigzag stitch and matching or contrasting thread to stitch along the outside edge of each warp and weft strip.

I used this technique to add color and texture to the unevenly cut edges of my jacket "Pink Razzle" (page 57).

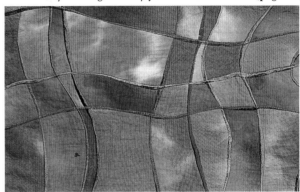

*Zigzag over cut edges to add more dimension to your woven and quilted yardage.*

**Q:** *Now that I have finished my woven and quilted jacket, I've decided it's too plain and I want to add double-welt pockets. Since the backing is my lining, which would normally be added last to cover the pocket construction inside, how do I add a pocket?*

**A:** First, make the welt pocket as you would a large bound buttonhole. Cut a piece of backing fabric (or other fabric of your choice) for the inside pocket. Turn under and press all raw edges and pin in place over the welts on the inside of the garment. Whipstitch in place. You won't want to put heavy, bulky items in the finished pockets, but the added detail on the right side is worth it. I used this technique on "Blue Checks Out" (page 62).

*Welt pocket detailing*　　　*A pocket patch on the inside covers the pocket construction.*

## CHAPTER 5

# Three Sample Projects

Read through all the instructions first, experiment with some woven samples, color a weaving diagram, then gather your fabrics and follow along to make your own vest, simple jacket, or coat. When you've finished, you'll see how easy it is to apply these directions to other projects in the book or to your own designs.

## SUMMER DREAMIN'

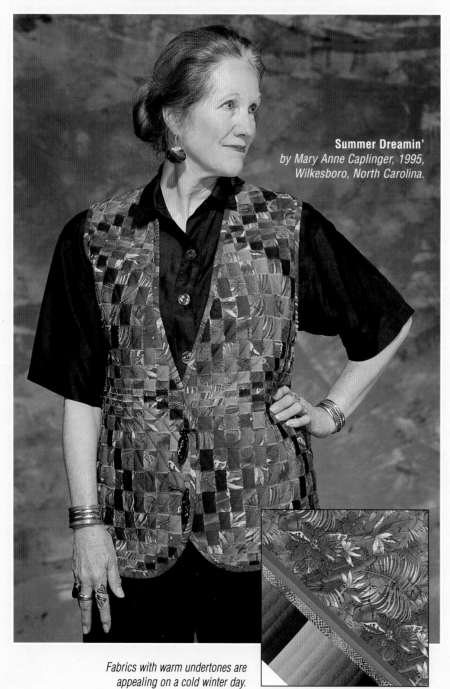

**Summer Dreamin'**
*by Mary Anne Caplinger, 1995, Wilkesboro, North Carolina.*

*Fabrics with warm undertones are appealing on a cold winter day.*

For this vest, I chose the fabrics, then developed the weaving pattern to focus on the stripes. Once these decisions were made, I could see that the color and pattern would be the strongest elements in this garment. Also, any repeat pattern made with the striped fabric would cover a fairly large area. An entire jacket might be overwhelming; a simple, somewhat longer vest was the best shape to use.

On a dark and dreary winter day, while browsing in a fabric store, I spotted the bright tropical floral fabric. A quilted garment made with the lush green leaves and bright flowers promised to add warmth—literally and figuratively—to the basic black pieces in my winter wardrobe. The color-coordinated, graduated-stripe fabric offered intriguing design possibilities.

The samples at right show some patterns that are easy to create by cutting strips in different widths or moving them in different sequences.

These experiments were fun to do and, as a result, I now look at striped fabrics from a new perspective. If you have some ombré, or graduated-color, fabrics in your collection, pull them out and try a few samples. You'll see how simple it is to create the look of plaid or a wave.

The samples also showed how the strips need to be torn from different areas in the striped fabric or pieced to maintain a repeat pattern.

I considered each of the samples and finally settled on the staggered-wave repeat for this vest. Also, by tearing the strips in graduated widths, I could mimic the look of Bargello.

Next, I colored a weaving diagram to check the repeat and calculate the size and number of weft strips. I'm glad that I didn't skip this step because the colored diagram showed a potentially unflattering horizontal emphasis from the changing width of the strips. Accents of red and turquoise and a small-scale print in the warp break up the pattern and counter the horizontal design with a strong vertical line.

*(Top) Torn weft strips are staggered to form a wave pattern.*
*(Bottom) Bias-cut weft strips are staggered to create the illusion of asymmetrical triangles.*

*(Top) Torn warp and weft strips are placed to create a softly shaded square.*
*(Bottom) Torn warp and weft strips alternate light and dark strips in an ikat-inspired traditional weaver's Log Cabin pattern.*

WEAVING DIAGRAM

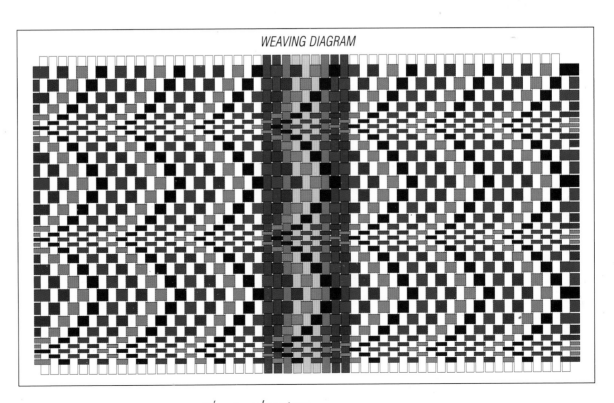

Three Sample Projects

## Materials (44"-wide fabrics)

Yardage given is for size 10; other sizes may require more or less yardage. Tear all fabrics, except the graduated stripe, across the fabric width (crosswise grain). Tear the stripe along the lengthwise grain.

2 yds. floral print
2 yds. green graduated stripe
¼ yd. red solid
¼ yd. turquoise solid
¼ yd. small-scale print
1½ yds. Thermore batting
1½ yds. red China silk or silky polyester for lining
Quilting thread in black, dark blue-green, medium green, and light green

## Cutting

For garments larger than size 10, you may need to add warp or weft strips and cut larger pieces for lining and batting.

| Fabric | Used For | No. of Pieces | Size |
|---|---|---|---|
| Floral print | Warp | 54 | 1" x 34" |
| | Bias binding | 1 | 2" x 100" |
| | | 1 | 2" x 30" |
| | | 2 | 2" x 30" |
| Green stripe | Weft | 8 | 1½" x 54" |
| | | 5 | 1¼" x 54" |
| | | 5 | 1" x 54" |
| | | 6 | ¾" x 54" |
| | | 9 | ½" x 54" |
| Red solid | Warp | 4 | 1" x 34" |
| Turquoise | Warp | 2 | 1" x 34" |
| Small print | Warp | 3 | 1" x 34" |
| Batting | | 1 | 34" x 54" |
| Red silk | Backing | 1 | 34" x 54" |

## Preparing the Pattern

Use the vest pattern on the pullout at the back of the book or a commercial pattern of similar styling.

1. Select fabrics and decide on the weaving pattern that you will use. Trace the pattern in the appropriate size onto tracing paper or pattern tracing cloth. The pattern is given in two pieces that must be joined at the underarm to create a one-piece pattern with front and back combined. See additional directions on the pullout pattern.

2. Make a muslin to check the fit of the pattern. See "Checking the Fit—Making a Muslin" on page 14. As mentioned previously, a test sample is very important to the success of your garment.

   My sample vest showed slight gaps at the front armholes and neckline. I marked these areas with pins. Since I didn't want darts, I planned to take up the extra fabric with ease stitching. Ease stitching is a row of long basting stitches in the seam allowance that is pulled up slightly to control the excess fullness.

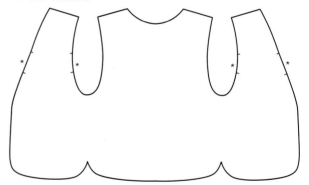

\* Control too much fullness in
the marked areas with easestitching.

3. Transfer the final alterations from the muslin to the paper pattern for a permanent reference. Remember that if you want to cut a flat piece of fabric, the pattern piece must also lie flat. Be sure to taper the edges of any tucks or slashes you made across the pattern until it lies flat.

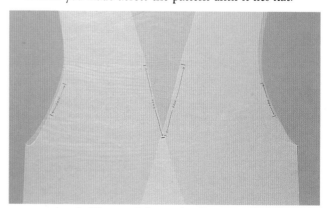

*I marked the areas to be eased on the paper pattern.*

# Weaving the Yardage and Quilting

1. Use the individual pattern pieces to determine the dimensions of the backing and batting for each piece. (See "Preparing to Weave" on page 19.) It is important to cut these oversize to allow for take-up during quilting.

   Measure the paper pattern at its longest and widest points and add 4" to each measurement. This will give you the dimensions for the working size. Four inches is the minimum take-up allowance; I added 4" more to the width of this vest because it's an exceptionally wide piece.

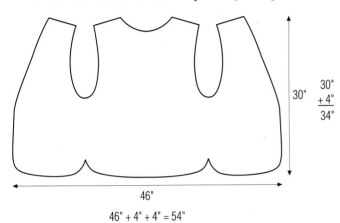

30"
30"
+ 4"
34"

46"

46" + 4" + 4" = 54"

Cut backing and batting: 34" x 54"

2. Cut the backing and batting.
3. Pin or tape the backing, right side down, to your work surface. Place the batting on top of the backing and anchor it in place.

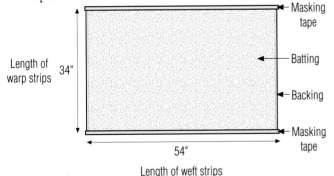

Length of warp strips  34"

Masking tape

Batting

Backing

Masking tape

54"

Length of weft strips

4. Prepare the warp strips. Tear or cut and press the required number of strips, following the weaving diagram. (The required number for size 10 or smaller is given in the chart on page 40.) The warp strips for "Summer Dreamin'" are 1" wide throughout to keep the focus on the weft, and 34" long, the same length as the backing.
5. Lay the vertical warp strips, right side up, in sequence across the batting. To keep the warp straight and provide the right amount of tension, use straight pins or tape to secure the strips at the upper and lower edges. Check to make sure all the warp strips are snug against each other, not overlapping.

*Arrange the vertical warp strips in the desired sequence.*

6. Prepare the weft strips. Measure the width of the backing to determine the length of the weft strips. Tear or cut and press the weft strips as you did the warp. You may need to piece the weft strips for the proper length. (See "Changing Strips in Mid-row" on page 26.) The weft strips for "Summer Dreamin'" are 54" long.

   The weft strips may be any width you choose. The Bargello effect in the weaving pattern for this vest is enhanced by using strips of five different widths: 1½", 1¼", 1", ¾", and ½".

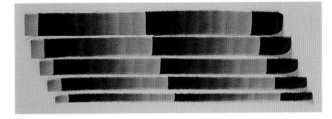

*Adjust the weft strip placement to create a Bargello pattern in the finished piece.*

7. Begin weaving the weft strips. Starting at the top, pick up a weft strip and slide it under every other warp strip. You will quickly develop the "over one, under one" rhythm. When you reach the opposite edge, hold each end in your fingers; pull the strip taut to make it lie straight and flat.

   Lay your rotary ruler on top of the strip and adjust any areas that are not straight. Pin each end of the strip to the batting and backing.

   Weave the second weft strip, reversing the "over one, under one" pattern. The second weft strip lies on top of each warp strip that the first weft strip went under—easier done than said!

8. Continue weaving the remaining weft strips in sequence, smoothing and straightening the warp strips as you go. After every other weft strip, use your rotary ruler to make sure the warp and weft are straight and perpendicular to each other.

If you're not comfortable weaving with your fingers, use a weaving or craft needle. You can also make your own needle. (See "Weaving & Sewing Tools" on page 16.)

9. While the weaving is still taped to the work surface, place pins in the center of each intersection of warp and weft strips to pin-baste for quilting. After the entire piece is pinned, remove the tape.

To emphasize the Bargello patterning of my vest, I machine quilted with a straight stitch, following the curve of the color bars.

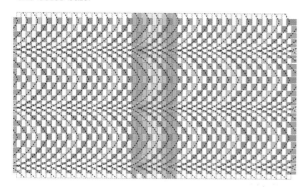

As a result, every intersection is not stitched. This is not recommended for a garment that will be washed often, but since the vest will always be worn over a shirt, it won't have to be washed after every wearing.

## Cutting, Assembling & Finishing

1. Refer to step 1 in "Cutting & Assembling the Pieces" on page 30 to cut out the vest.
2. Using a basting-length stitch, easestitch ½" from the seam line between the marks on the vest front and front armhole edges for shaping and to draw the edges in slightly to fit your curves. Backstitch at the beginning of the ease stitching to anchor it securely, but do not backstitch at the end of the ease stitching.

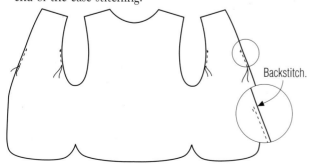

Backstitch.

3. With right sides together, stitch the shoulder seams and finish with a flat-felled seam as shown on page 31.

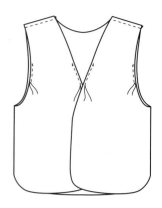

4. Draw up the ease stitching to remove approximately ⅜" of fullness at each front and armhole edge. Try the vest on and adjust the gathers if necessary for a smooth fit. The front edges should gently cup in over the bustline curve, and the armhole should fit smoothly without gapping. Be careful not to draw up too much ease, creating a "pooch" at the edge or a "bubble" in the garment. To anchor the threads, place a pin in the garment at the end of the stitching and wrap the thread around it in a figure eight.

Draw up easestitching.

5. Remove the vest and tie the threads in a secure dressmaker's knot.
6. Choose a fabric to bind the outer edges. It can be one you used for the weaving or a contrasting fabric. Cut 4 separate bias strips for the vest in the lengths given below:

Back: 1 strip, 2" x 30", for the bottom edge, from the inside points of the curves
Armholes: 2 strips, each 2" x 30"
Front: 1 strip, 2" x 100", to reach around the neckline and front edges and up to the inside of the curve at the sides; join strips as shown on page 33 to obtain the required length.

7. Apply the binding to the raw edges as shown in "Binding" on page 33. When you apply it to areas that have been eased to fit, adjust the fullness evenly along the ease stitching and use several pins to secure it for stitching. If you are full-busted and have drawn in more than ⅜", you can try steaming the eased areas with the tip of your iron to shrink in the fullness.

To bind the inner points and curves at the lower side edges of the vest:

a. Following the diagram, make a triangular stay from a small piece of backing fabric.

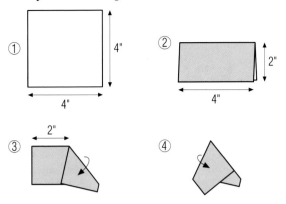

Folding the Triangular Stay

b. Position the stay with the point of the triangle on the inside of the vest, placing it 1" above the inner point of the curve. Hand baste the two long sides in place. Trim the excess to match the curve.

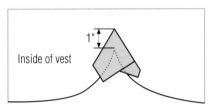

Hand sew stay over inner point of curve.

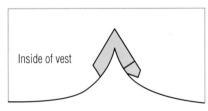

Trim stay to match curve of vest.

c. On the wrong side of the garment, lightly draw intersecting seam lines at the side seam curves.

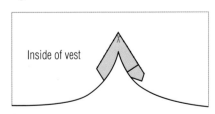

Mark ⅜"-wide seam line.

d. Beginning with the short raw edge of the binding strip, ¼" above the inner point of the side-seam curve, pin the front binding piece in place, right sides together and raw edges even. Push a pin through the point where the seam lines (the lines you drew) intersect, and mark it with a dot on the wrong side of the binding as shown above right. Pin the remainder of the binding strip in place, ending at the opposite side-seam curve and marking a

dot there in the same manner. Stitch from dot to dot, ⅜" from the raw edges.

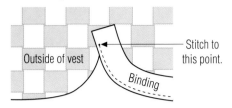

e. Fold the binding at an angle as shown.

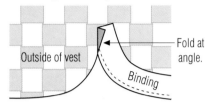

f. Fold binding a second time.

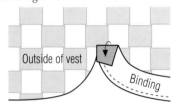

g. Turn the binding to the inside of the garment and fold under the raw edge so that the fold just covers the stitching. Press carefully and pin-baste. Hand stitch the binding to the garment lining so the stitches don't show on the front or the back.

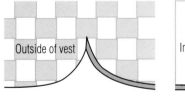 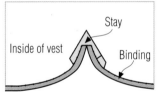

Fold binding to inside.          Sew binding in place.

h. On the right side of the garment, slipstitch the edges of the binding in place at the point.

i. Bind the bottom edge of the back in the same way.

8. Select a button or other embellishment for a closure if desired. On my vest, I sewed 2 large, leaf-shaped beads to the right front and added small, functional snaps underneath for a simple closure.

*The unique closure adds a finishing touch.*

# TUXEDO VEST

This short, tuxedo-style vest made from men's neckties is a versatile topper. Whether you wear the vest over jeans or dressy slacks, the red and black figured silks in a braided pattern add a dash of color and texture. It's fun to shop at flea markets and secondhand stores for ties to make this vest. But don't go shopping in your sweetie's closet without his permission. He won't be happy when his favorite ties disappear only to reappear in your new vest! Of course, you can substitute other fabrics to make this vest if ties are unavailable.

Simple machine stitching follows the twill weave for a functional, understated quilting method. Designer labels from the ties were hand appliquéd to the front and back of the vest.

**Tuxedo Vest**
*by Mary Anne Caplinger,*
*1995, Wilkesboro,*
*North Carolina.*

*Quilting follows the weave pattern in "Tuxedo Vest."*

*WEAVING DIAGRAM*

## Materials *(44"-wide fabrics and men's neckties)*

Yardage and number of ties are given for standard size 10. Other sizes may require more or less yardage and ties. Cut the warp and weft strips from the ties. The number of strips that you can cut from each tie may vary, depending on the condition (avoid worn areas) and width of the tie.

20 red men's neckties (stripes and prints)
20 black men's neckties (stripes and prints)
1½ yds. black silk noil for lining and binding
1 purchased frog closure
Quilting thread in red and black

## Cutting

For garments larger than size 10, you may need to add warp or weft strips and cut larger pieces for lining and batting.

| Fabric | Used For | No. of Pieces | Size |
|---|---|---|---|
| Red ties | Warp | 20 | 1" x 36" |
| | | 40 | 1" x 24" |
| Black ties | Weft | 20 | 1" x 36" |
| | | 40 | 1" x 24" |
| Black silk | Back lining | 1 | 23" x 24" |
| | Front lining | 1 | 26" x 30" |
| | Binding | 1 | 1¾" x 97" |
| | | 2 | 1¾" x 27" |

## Preparing the Ties and Pattern

Use the full-size vest pattern on the pullout at the back of the book or a commercial pattern of similar styling. *The pattern on the pullout is slightly longer and looser fitting than the one in the photo on page 44.*

1. Collect old ties from friends or thrift stores and sort them by color. Choose subtle prints and unobtrusive stripes so individual strips don't detract from the braided effect.

   Remove the label, undo the stitching in the center seam, and remove the interfacing in each tie. (Set aside the interfacing for making new ties if you wish, or give it to a friend who makes ties.) Save some of the labels to appliqué on the finished vest if desired.

2. Using tracing paper and a pencil, trace the pattern pieces in the appropriate size. Use the pieces to cut a test garment from medium-weight cotton or muslin. Machine baste the pieces together and check the fit. Transfer any alterations to the paper pattern.

## Weaving the Yardage and Quilting

Refer to "Weaving" on page 24.

1. Press the ties to remove creases. Using a rotary cutter and ruler, cut 1"-wide strips along the lengthwise center of each tie. You may be able to cut more than one strip from a very wide tie.

   **NOTE:** Since ties are made from bias-cut fabric, the strips won't ravel. They will stretch, however, so handle them carefully.

   Not all the strips you cut will be long enough for the total warp and weft length needed for a vest. You'll need to piece some strips with matching or similar colors. (See "Changing Strips in Mid-row" on page 26.)

2. This vest is constructed *without batting.* You'll weave the strips on top of the backing (lining of the vest). Measure the back pattern piece at its longest and widest points. Add 4" to each measurement for the working size of the back piece. Cut the back piece from the backing fabric. (See pages 24–25.)

   Cut the backing for the two fronts as one larger piece. To figure the dimensions for this piece, see page 24. For a size 10, I cut the backing 26" x 30" for the fronts and 23" x 24" for the back. These pieces should be slightly larger for each step up in size.

3. Place the backing piece for the front, right side down, on your work surface and secure with masking tape or pins. Place the first warp strip, right side up, on the backing at a 45° angle to the top and bottom edges of the backing. Pin the ends in place. Continue adding warp strips, checking often to make sure the 45° angle is maintained.

Laying Warp Strips at 45° Angle

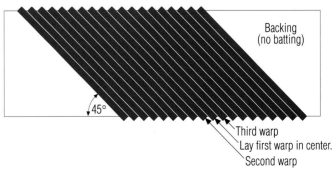

Backing (no batting)

45°

Third warp
Lay first warp in center.
Second warp

4. Begin at the center, weaving the weft strips in and out of the warp strips, following the weaving diagram. Notice that the braided effect is a result of the twill weave—"over three, under three."

   Since the bias-cut silk tie fabrics stretch easily, be careful not to pull the strips as taut as you would if using torn cotton strips. Lay the strips flat and snug against each other; pin at each end. After every other weft row, align the strips with your rotary ruler, making sure that the 45° angle is maintained. Adjust strips as needed.

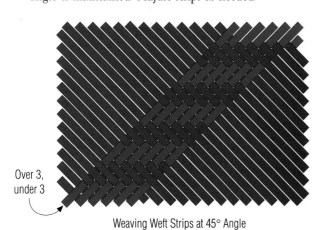

Over 3, under 3

Weaving Weft Strips at 45° Angle

5. Decide how you want to quilt the woven yardage. Because the vest is short and the weaving pattern is bold, it's probably best to choose a simple quilting design that follows the strips. Pin-baste well to control the slippery fabric strips. Quilt by hand or machine as desired.

   For the vest pictured, I quilted with straight machine stitching, following the zigzag line of the strips, alternating black and red thread from row to row.

6. Repeat steps 3–5 to make the piece for the vest back.

## Cutting, Assembling & Finishing

1. Press the completed yardage and cut out the vest pieces.
2. With right sides together and following the directions for "Flat-Felled Seams" on page 31, stitch the shoulder and side seams.

Inside of vest

Stitch seams right sides together.
Use flat-felled seams (page 31).

3. Staystitch and cut away the ⅝"-wide seam allowances along the armhole, neckline, front, and bottom edges as shown on page 33.
4. Beginning at the lower left side seam and following the directions for "Binding" on page 33, apply the binding to the outer edges of the vest. Bind the armhole edges in the same manner.
5. Select a few labels that color-coordinate with your woven strips. Hand sew the labels at random to the vest back and fronts.
6. Sew the frog closure at the mark indicated on the pattern.
7. Wear your new vest and enjoy!

# Amish Logs Coat

Welcome cool weather in a long, quilted cotton coat inspired by the color palette of favorite Amish quilts. The strips are woven in a playful version of the traditional weaver's Log Cabin pattern. Four different widths of cotton strips combine with black to produce a bold design of alternating colors in the warp and weft. A shawl collar frames the face and extends into narrow lapels for a slimming, single-breasted opening. Use this pattern for a shorter jacket if you prefer.

**Amish Logs Coat**
*by Mary Anne Caplinger, 1995, Wilkesboro, North Carolina.*

### WEAVING DIAGRAM

*Quilting in a variety of colors and geometric patterns creates a subtle layer of activity on the surface of the woven grid.*

Three Sample Projects

## Materials *(44"-wide fabrics)*

Yardage given is for size 10; other sizes may require more or less yardage.
Tear the warp and weft strips across the fabric width (crosswise grain).

4 yds. black cotton
2 yds. blue-purple cotton
1¼ yds. khaki cotton
1 yd. dark teal cotton
1 yd. magenta cotton

4¾ yds. Thermore batting
4¾ yds. black China-silk for coat lining
Quilting thread (rayon) in black, teal,
blue-purple, khaki, and magenta

3 buttons, ¾" or 1" diameter
Purchased shoulder pads

## Cutting

For garments larger than size 10, you may need to add warp
or weft strips and cut larger pieces for lining and batting.

| Fabric | Used For | | No. of Pieces | Size |
|---|---|---|---|---|
| Black cotton | Warp | (Back) | 6 | 1½" x 51" |
| | | | 3 | 1" x 51" |
| | | | 3 | ¾" x 51" |
| | | | 3 | ½" x 51" |
| | | (Sleeves) | 6 | 1½" x 51" |
| | | | 3 | 1" x 51" |
| | | | 3 | ¾" x 51" |
| | | | 3 | ½" x 51" |
| | | (Fronts) | 7 | 1½" x 59" |
| | | | 3 | 1" x 59" |
| | | | 3 | ¾" x 59" |
| | | | 3 | ½" x 59" |
| | Weft | (Back) | 6 | 1½" x 28" |
| | | | 8 | 1" x 28" |
| | | | 6 | ¾" x 28" |
| | | | 6 | ½" x 28" |
| | | (Sleeves) | 6 | 1½" x 28" |
| | | | 8 | 1" x 28" |
| | | | 6 | ¾" x 28" |
| | | | 6 | ½" x 28" |
| | | (Fronts) | 8 | 1½" x 34" |
| | | | 8 | 1" x 34" |
| | | | 6 | ¾" x 34" |
| | | | 6 | ½" x 34" |
| Blue-purple | Warp | (Back) | 5 | 1½" x 51" |
| | | (Sleeves) | 5 | 1½" x 51" |
| | | (Fronts) | 6 | 1½" x 59" |

| Fabric | Used For | | No. of Pieces | Size |
|---|---|---|---|---|
| Blue-purple | Weft | (Back) | 6 | 1½" x 28" |
| | | (Sleeves) | 6 | 1½" x 28" |
| (cont.) | | (Fronts) | 7 | 1½" x 32" |
| Khaki | Warp | (Back) | 3 | 1" x 55" |
| | | (Sleeves) | 3 | 1" x 51" |
| | | (Fronts) | 3 | 1" x 51" |
| | Weft | (Back) | 8 | 1" x 28" |
| | | (Sleeves) | 8 | 1" x 28" |
| | | (Fronts) | 7 | 1" x 34" |
| Dark teal | Warp | (Back) | 3 | ¾" x 51" |
| | | (Sleeves) | 3 | ¾" x 51" |
| | | (Fronts) | 6 | ¾" x 59" |
| | Weft | (Back) | 6 | ¾" x 28" |
| | | (Sleeves) | 6 | ¾" x 28" |
| | | (Fronts) | 6 | ¾" x 34" |
| Magenta | Warp | (Back) | 3 | ½" x 51" |
| | | (Sleeves) | 3 | ½" x 51" |
| | | (Fronts) | 3 | ½" x 59" |
| | Weft | (Back) | 6 | ½" x 28" |
| | | (Sleeves) | 6 | ½" x 28" |
| | | (Fronts) | 6 | ½" x 34" |
| Batting | Back | | 1 | 28" x 51" |
| | Sleeves | | 1 | 28" x 51" |
| | Fronts | | 1 | 34" x 59" |
| Black silk | Back lining | | 1 | 28" x 51" |
| | Sleeve lining | | 1 | 34" x 50" |
| | Front lining | | 1 | 34" x 50" |

(For bias binding, see step 5 on page 50.)

## Preparing the Pattern

Use the coat pattern on the pullout at the back of the book or a commercial pattern of similar styling. *There are no hem allowances included at the bottom edge or on the sleeves. All edges are bound.* Refer to the size chart on the pullout.

1. Using tracing paper and a pencil, trace the pattern pieces in the appropriate size. Use the pieces to cut a test garment from inexpensive quilted cotton fabric. (See "Checking the Fit—Making a Muslin" on page 14.)
2. Machine baste the muslin, using ¾"-wide seam allowances throughout. Stitch the fronts to the back at the shoulders.

3. With right sides together, sew the short ends of the collar together.

4. Sew the collar to the back neckline, matching notches and circles. Cut 4 small V-shaped notches in the back neckline seam allowance if necessary.

5. Set the sleeves into the open armhole, matching the shoulder dot to the shoulder seam. Pin-baste liberally, distributing any fullness evenly.

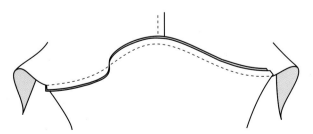

6. Stitch the sleeve and side seams in one continuous seam.

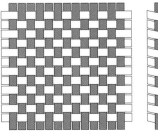

7. Try on the test garment, insert shoulder pads, and adjust the fit as needed. Make sure to adjust the sleeve and bottom length to the desired finished length, since you will be binding the raw edges rather than hemming them. Transfer any alterations to the paper pattern.

## Weaving the Yardage and Quilting

1. Measure the back pattern piece at its longest and widest points for the dimensions of the backing and batting. Add 4" to each measurement and cut the backing and batting to size. (See "Weaving" on page 24.) Secure the backing and batting to your work surface.
2. Prepare the warp and weft strips. You'll need to piece the warp strips for the proper length. The total length of the warp strips given in the chart is longer than actually needed; this allows you the flexibility to move the strips in the weaving to hide the joining points under the weft strips. (See "Changing Strips in Mid-row" on page 26.)
3. Beginning with the front piece, lay warp strips on the batting in the order shown in the weaving diagram on page 47. The weaving diagram is wide enough so you can follow it to weave the two fronts as one piece, then cut them out. You may not need to use the entire width for the back or sleeve pieces. Straighten the strips and anchor the upper and lower edges with tape or pins.
4. Referring to "Weaving" on page 24, begin weaving the weft strips in and out of the warp strips, following the weaving diagram. Check the alignment of the strips every other row, using your rotary ruler. This is especially important when weaving a large piece, since it is common for the strips to gradually drift down, creating an undesirable finished piece.

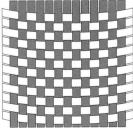

5. When you have finished weaving the front piece, pin-baste the layers together for quilting. (See "Marking and Basting the Layers" on page 26.)

6. Mark the quilting lines, if needed, one section at a time. You may need to reposition the basting pins as you mark and quilt.

7. Quilt one section at a time, removing pins as you come to them. If necessary, clean-finish the beginning and ending points of your quilting lines for a neat appearance on the reverse side.

8. Weave the back in the same manner as you did the front. Weave the sleeve and pocket yardage in one large piece, measuring the sleeve pattern on the diagonal to determine how large to cut the backing piece. Mark, baste, and quilt as you did for the fronts.

NOTE: After I wove each coat section, I turned it over and scattered leftover weaving strips in random fashion on the backing side for a designer touch. I fused these in place with fusible web, then completed the quilting from the right side. I removed the basting pins from each place temporarily before I fused the strips, then replaced them immediately.

*Leftovers add a touch of color and texture to the inside of the coat.*

## Cutting, Assembling & Finishing

1. Lightly press each completed piece, then cut the garment pieces from the yardage. When cutting the fronts, remember to cut a right and a left front. Position the pattern piece and cut the fronts as if you were cutting the pieces from a plaid, aligning the weft strips to match across the center front. Cut the sleeves from the yardage on the diagonal, making sure to cut a right and left sleeve. Cut the pocket from the leftover sleeve yardage.

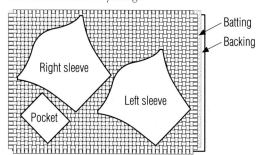

2. Referring to "Flat-Felled Seams" on page 31, sew the fronts to the back at the shoulders and sew the collar sections together as shown for making the test garment in steps 2 and 3 of "Preparing the Pattern" on page 49. Sew the collar to the back neckline (step 4) using the same seam finish.

3. Sew the sleeve to the open armhole as shown in step 5 on page 49. To finish the sleeve seam edge, trim it to ½" and bind the seam edge by hand with a strip of 2"-wide bias binding cut from leftover backing fabric. Turn the seam toward the sleeve.

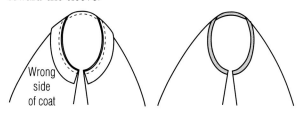

*Sew binding to armhole seam allowance.*

4. Use a flat-felled seam to sew the fronts to the backs at the side seams.

5. To finish all outer edges of the coat and the pocket edges, cut 3"-wide bias strips from the leftover fabrics. I used one color for the front and collar edges and a different color for each sleeve edge. I also changed colors along the bottom edge so that the back and each front bottom edge were bound in a different color. Attach the binding to each raw edge of the coat as shown in "Binding" on page 33, using a ⅝"-wide seam allowance.

   Bind all four edges of the pocket, mitering the corners as shown on page 34. Be sure to stop stitching ⅝" from each corner before you stitch the miter.

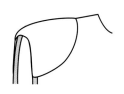

*Miter the binding corners.*

6. Position the pocket on the right coat front and slipstitch in place.

7. Try on the coat, insert the shoulder pads, and pin in place. The outer edge of the pad should extend ½" beyond the armhole *seam line*. Adjust the pad position if necessary, remove the coat, and hand sew the shoulder pads in place along shoulder seams at corners.

*Shoulder pad extends beyond armhole seam line.*

8. Make 3 buttonholes on the right front as marked on the pattern. If you adjusted the coat length, reposition the buttonholes. Sew the buttons in place on the left front.

9. Wear and enjoy the compliments that are sure to come your way!

## CHAPTER 6

# Design Portfolio

Movement creates energy, and that's what Bonnie Berlin had in mind for this lively and playful vest. She wanted to "hear" the rhythms of the changing colors as she looked at the transition between warm and cool in the weaving. Random widths of hand-painted silk in plain weave continue the beat as colors converge at the intersection of warp and weft strips.

In keeping with the lighthearted spirit, the outside edges were left unfinished except for a double row of zigzag stitching. A soft fringe of knots around the lower edge, formed by tying every two warp strips together, completes a vest that is fun to look at and fun to wear.

## COLOR RHYTHMS

Color Rhythms by Bonnie Berlin, 1995, Winston-Salem, North Carolina.

*WEAVING DIAGRAM*

*Back view of "Color Rhythms"*

# GLITTERATI

**Glitterati**
*by Christine Barnes, 1994,*
*Grass Valley, California.*

WEAVING DIAGRAM

Random stitching in cotton, rayon, and metallic thread lends sparkle and sophistication to this holiday bolero vest by Christine Barnes. "First you weave the unwashed fabric strips, then stitch till you drop!" Christine says. Washing and drying the woven and stitched piece before you cut out the vest gives it a crinkly look.

For this look, it's essential to use all-cotton fabric. Don't use decorator fabrics or cotton/polyester blends—they won't shrink and crinkle during washing and drying. To avoid fading, wash in warm water and dry on medium heat. If the piece isn't crinkly enough, wash it again in hot water and dry on high heat.

After weaving, stitch the woven piece in all directions using various threads. It's easiest to stitch uniformly with one thread color, then change thread and do roughly the same amount of stitching. Stitch in straight lines or curves—the decision is yours—and cover the entire piece. As the stitching becomes denser, fill in areas that have less stitching.

Some machines get hot with nonstop use, so it's a good idea to feel your bobbin periodically and rest your machine if necessary.

# MIDNIGHT PASSION

Deep, rich, saturated color transforms plain white silk into a visual feast. Red, blue, green, gold, and purple dyes brushed onto pleated fabric migrate and blend into new shades and tones of the original colors.

A herringbone twill weave highlights the textural contrast between the luster of China silk and the matte surface of silk crepe de chine. Machine quilting emphasizes the diagonal movement created by the rhythmic spacing of the weft strips. The woven yardage is quilted to thin, lightweight batting without backing. The black silk lining was added separately to conceal shoulder pads. Black piping and flat trim outline the edges for a crisp finish.

**Midnight Passion**
*by Mary Anne Caplinger, 1994, Wilkesboro, North Carolina.*

### WEAVING DIAGRAM

*The hand-dyed fabric achieves its painterly look from a random application of dyes after it was folded in accordion pleats.*

# JAPANESE FANTASY GARDEN

A simple cardigan takes on a new persona when made from brightly colored woven and quilted yardage. Barbara Weiland chose the Japanese cotton print in some of her favorite colors, then added a variety of coordinating prints. For construction, she chose a plain weave with random color placement. Beads from a discarded necklace create a front "yoke" for added texture. Sleeves cut from the original fabric preserve the design and add visual contrast to the textured jacket body. Assorted yarns, softly twisted together and hand tacked along the inner edge of the binding and at the armhole seam, add a finishing flourish.

**Japanese Fantasy Garden**
*by Barbara Weiland, 1995,
Redmond, Washington.*

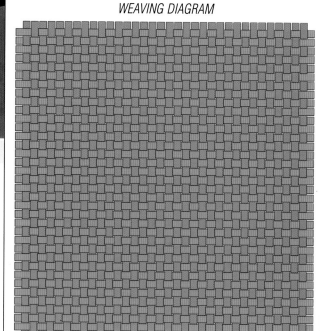

*Seed beads create a yoke, and twisted cord accents the bound edges of this simple-to-sew jacket.*

*WEAVING DIAGRAM*

A favorite for traveling, this jacket has a secret. It is lined with a resist-dyed purple lining, making it completely reversible. Rib-knit banding, front zipper, and welt pockets characterize the casual bomber style, making it versatile and comfortable to wear.

Strips torn from five different fabrics were chosen at random and woven in an open plain weave on a black cotton background. The small, black accent squares function as a repeat pattern, giving continuity to the mix of patterned fabrics.

The yardage for the jacket was woven on and quilted to a thin, lightweight batting without a backing fabric. The quilting lines follow the warp and weft for a subtle grid pattern, keeping the focus on the printed fabrics. After the weaving and quilting were finished, the lining was attached by machine around the neck, cuffs, and lower edge. The jacket was turned right side out, and the front edges of the lining were carefully hand sewn to the zipper tape. On a trip, this jacket easily moves from casual to dressy with a flip of the wrist.

**Purplefest**
by Mary Anne Caplinger, 1992,
Wilkesboro, North Carolina.

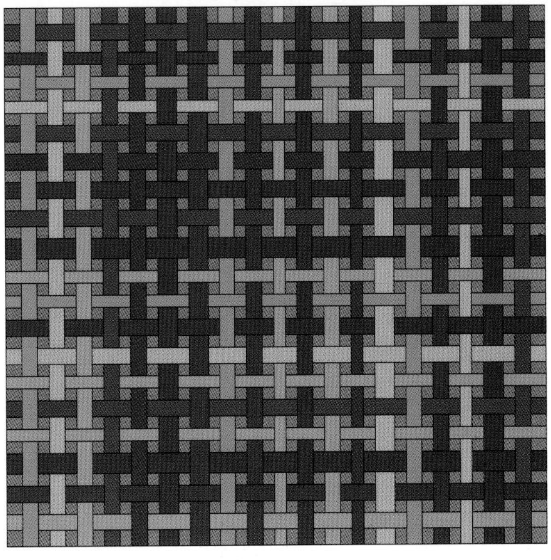

Narrow white diagonals and complementary colors of gold and terra cotta enliven the dark purple and turquoise prints in this versatile jacket.

**WEAVING DIAGRAM**

Design Portfolio

# SHADOW WALTZ

The challenge: design a woven and quilted jacket for a banking executive to wear to work. The response: one striking cotton batik fabric in subdued neutrals, torn and manipulated to form a lively graphic design, produced a conservative but spirited answer to the challenge.

Quilting lines in a free-form wave echo the fabric's hand-drawn feather pattern and counter the sharp diagonal steps of the herringbone weave.

Twisted black cord was hand sewn to the edges of the collar, pockets, and jacket front.

With a change from turtleneck and slacks to silk blouse and skirt, the tailored jacket goes from casual to business functions and beyond.

**Shadow Waltz**
*by Mary Anne Caplinger, 1995,
Wilkesboro, North Carolina.*

*Wide strips shading from light
to dark emphasize the twill
weave in a classic jacket.*

### WEAVING DIAGRAM

Clouds of emerald, teal, and magenta float across this jacket, broken into abstract shapes by the crossing of warp and weft strips. Full-strength, fiber-reactive dyes brushed at random onto damp white cotton produced puddles of high contrast between dyed and undyed areas. The wide, undulating strips disguise a simple plain-weave structure woven on a cotton backing without batting. To imitate this look, cut the wavy warp and weft strips and keep them in their cut order when weaving.

Meandering lines of satin stitch in shiny rayon and silk threads cover the raw edges and contrast with the hand-dyed cotton. To balance the flat-woven jacket body, small tabs of the cotton, folded and attached by hand, embellish the sleeves and collar and outline the pockets, which were cleverly engineered along the edge of a vertical strip in each jacket front. This jacket steals the show. The textured sleeves are irresistible to all who see them.

**Pink Razzle**
*by Mary Anne Caplinger, 1992, Wilkesboro, North Carolina.*

### WEAVING DIAGRAM

*With the machine set for a close zigzag, slowly turn the stitch-width dial back and forth during stitching to produce thick and thin lines of satin stitch, such as those shown above.*

# JEWELS IN MOTION

**Jewels in Motion**
by Bonnie Berlin, 1995,
Winston-Salem, North
Carolina.

For this jacket, Bonnie Berlin imagined creating two lengths of hand-painted silk, one superimposed upon the other. Visualizing where the colors would meet in the weaving, she planned the transition between them for a feeling of movement. On one length, blues flow into purple and back to blue; on the second length, greens gently merge with turquoise and blue, then return to the original green. The completed weaving is a delight to the eyes, with fluid masses of color in constant motion across the jacket surface.

Bonnie sprayed damp white silk with diluted textile paint, allowing it to flow and mix before drying. After heat setting, some of the silk was torn and woven on a base of lightweight batting and silk backing.

Straight-stitch machine quilting follows the steps of the woven twill structure. Free-motion machine quilting in rhythmic lines covers the plain sleeves, providing contrast to the angular pattern on the jacket body.

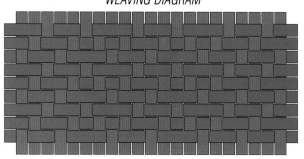

*WEAVING DIAGRAM*

# FEATHERS

The woven look goes casual in this ensemble of coordinated sweatshirt, T-shirt, and shorts. Cutting the center of the sweatshirt in a shallow V converted it from a pullover to a cardigan. A collar made from woven and quilted yardage surrounds the angled neckline, repeating colors from the shorts. Bias binding, created by piecing short lengths of the weaving fabrics, finishes the neck and front edges.

On the T-shirt, weft strips, torn from leftover shorts fabric, cross warp strips cut to form a yoke in the front and back of the shirt. I drew vertical lines ½" apart from the base of the yoke up to, but not through, the shoulder seam as a guide for the rotary cutter. Then I slipped a small cutting mat between the shirt front and back and cut one layer at a time. After weaving, I stitched the weft strips in place along the outer edges of the yoke and anchored them with fusible knit interfacing on the inside. Diagonal quilting lines in purple and turquoise reinforce the yoke.

**Feathers**
*by Mary Anne Caplinger, 1995,
Wilkesboro, North Carolina.*

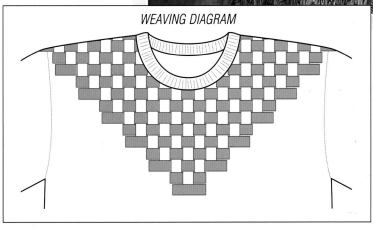

*WEAVING DIAGRAM*

# MOTHER-OF-THE-BRIDE COCOON

**Mother-of-the-Bride Cocoon**
*by Susan I. Jones, 1994,
Bellevue, Washington.*

A confection of chiffon, lace, and silk flowers enveloped the mother of the bride as she walked down the aisle in this commissioned work. Susan I. Jones wove strips of pastel chiffon on a base of lining fabric. Edges of the chiffon were finished with a rolled hem done on the serger. The wide lace collar extends over the sleeves and falls in soft folds at the back. Delicate roses of French wire ribbon encircle the neck and accentuate the waistline.

*Softly draped lace adds back appeal to this frothy jacket.*

*Serging controls the cut edges of the delicate chiffon in this exquisite jacket.*

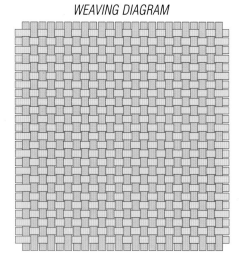

*WEAVING DIAGRAM*

Black satin ribbons, trimmed with a touch of gold metallic thread, embellish the bodice of this crepe blouse designed for a festive occasion. Decorative machine stitches in gold and black metallic threads add sparkly, graceful lines to the warp and weft. Ribbons applied to the crepe without a backing or batting highlight the contrast between the translucent fabric and the opaque trims.

Since the fabric was so soft, I planned the ribbon placement so the wider, firmer ribbons crossed at the center front of the yoke. Thinner, more flexible ribbons were used to continue the weaving pattern to the sides and lower edges of the blouse.

**Gold Dust**
by Mary Anne Caplinger, 1994,
Wilkesboro, North Carolina.

*WEAVING DIAGRAM*

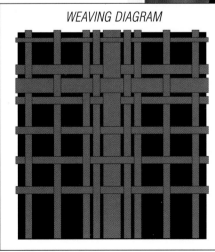

# BLUE CHECKS OUT

**Blue Checks Out**
*by Mary Anne Caplinger, 1992,
Wilkesboro, North Carolina.*

A great way to use leftovers! Small odd-shaped pieces of silk noil dictated cutting, rather than tearing the strips. Most warp and weft strips throughout this coat were pieced, some in more than one place. Threads escaping the cut edges add subtle texture to the surface.

The nubby silk noil, hand dyed in a narrow spectrum from blue to purple-brown to red, yielded strips of bright and subtle colors. The strips were placed to focus on areas of intense color. On the center right front and upper back, the warp and weft nearly match; on the upper left and lower back, a high-contrast checkerboard is formed by the red weft and blue warp.

Full sleeves, accented by widely spaced strips placed on the diagonal, gather into narrow woven cuffs.

The weaving diagram shows a section of the coat back with the mix of warp and weft sizes. The diagram is presented in solid colors for clarity. By its very nature, the coloration of each piece of hand-dyed cloth will be unique.

## WEAVING DIAGRAM

*Small squares of silk, embellished with beads, dot the yoke edge, repeating the basic grid shape of the weaving.*

Streams of honey and lemon with cream drift across the surface of this hand-dyed silk evening coat. Sharp accents of black add a strong graphic contrast to the random, painterly splotches of color.

The plain-weave grid, with warp and weft intersecting at right angles, gently imposes a sense of order and containment on the asymmetrical shapes. Spacing the warp and weft strips on a background of the same fabric reinforces the geometric weave structure and gives a sense of depth to the surface design.

The dramatic collar of hand-pleated warp and weft strips repeats the multidirectional movement of the colors, yet doesn't overwhelm because it remains confined to a small area.

**Lemon Lift**
by Mary Anne Caplinger, 1994, Wilkesboro, North Carolina.

*WEAVING DIAGRAM*

Short lengths of leftover warp and weft strips, pleated and hand stitched, completely cover the detachable collar.

Design Portfolio

# Earth, Wind, Fire & Water

This series began by reflecting on time as a dimension of space. The actual mathematical calculations elude me, but I've made a personal equation combining elements of textile history into contemporary garments that fill the space around me.

Ancient processes of dyeing and weaving silk join with contemporary machine embroidery in a timeless shape.

### Earth
*Wide strips of silk noil in subtle browns, greens, and golds form a background for embroidery. It recalls the sedimentary layers of the earth, prairie grasses, and rambling mountain ranges. Old buttons of vegetable ivory accent the closure.*

**Earth, Wind, Fire & Water**
*by Mary Anne Caplinger,
1991, Wilkesboro, North Carolina.*

### Wind
*Wispy edges on the torn strips of lightweight China silk give a feeling of movement to this representation of the wind. Strong diagonal quilting lines in silver metallic thread hint at the power of swiftly moving air.*

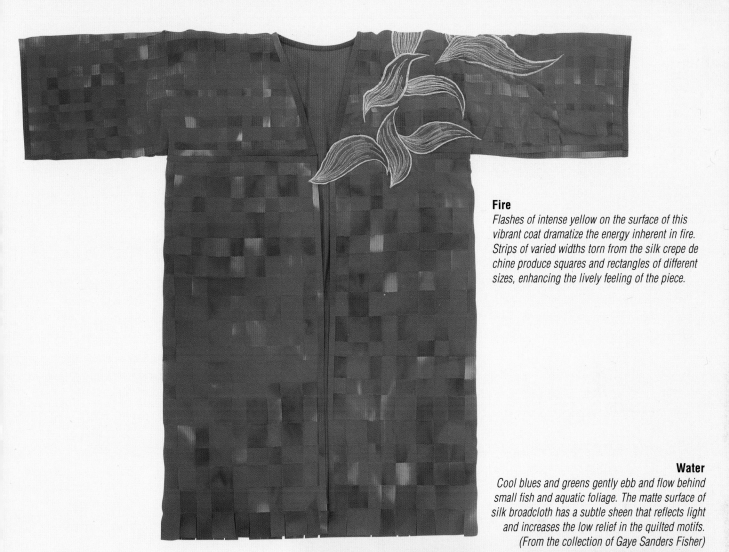

**Fire**

*Flashes of intense yellow on the surface of this vibrant coat dramatize the energy inherent in fire. Strips of varied widths torn from the silk crepe de chine produce squares and rectangles of different sizes, enhancing the lively feeling of the piece.*

**Water**

*Cool blues and greens gently ebb and flow behind small fish and aquatic foliage. The matte surface of silk broadcloth has a subtle sheen that reflects light and increases the low relief in the quilted motifs. (From the collection of Gaye Sanders Fisher)*

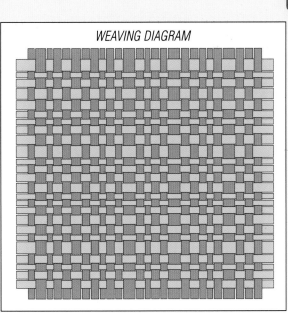

*WEAVING DIAGRAM*

Design Portfolio

## CHAPTER 7

# Lagniappe

Lagniappe (pronounced lan'yap) is a Creole word meaning "a little something extra," and that's just what this chapter offers. To whet your appetite for future exploration with the woven and quilted technique, I've pulled some weaving experiments from my idea file to share with you. There aren't any patterns to go along with these samples; they are for inspiration only, so have fun.

To test a variation in the woven and quilted process as it occurs to me, I often make a small sample of what I have in mind. I keep all samples together in a box for easy reference when I start a new project. You might want to begin a similar collection of samples.

Think about alternatives at each step of the process, from choosing fabrics to the final garment assembly. Ask yourself what would happen if you changed only one thing at each step, then make a sample illustrating that change. You will see how quickly one idea leads to another. Soon you will have a group of samples to remind you to try something new and different in your next project.

## CHANGING THE BASIC FABRIC

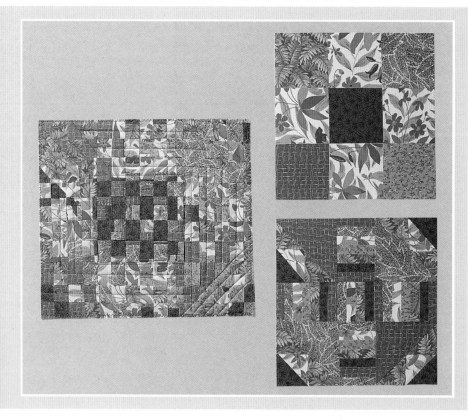

*To make a plain-weave pattern appear more complex, begin with pieced fabric. Sew together blocks left over from other projects, or piece a large Crazy-quilt block in the size you need. Cut warp strips from the pieced fabric and weave with whole fabric weft strips, either torn or cut. Alternatively, you can cut weft strips from pieced yardage too.*

Add texture to your woven and quilted garments by crinkling fabric before cutting or tearing it into strips. To crinkle the fabric, wet it, then gather it in loose, lengthwise folds, and twist in a figure eight. Allow to dry thoroughly. Tear strips from the dry, crinkled fabric, or apply lightweight fusible interfacing to the wrong side of the fabric, pressing gently but firmly enough so the interfacing adheres. Then, cut strips from the interfaced fabric. In the sample shown, a twill weave with long floats emphasizes the crinkled fabric.

Look for unusual open-weave fabrics to serve as warp or weft. I wove wide strips of black cotton between bands of colorful squares in this novelty fabric. The cotton strips add weight and stability to the base fabric. Next, I'll experiment with strips from fabric with a different hand—perhaps rayon challis or China silk.

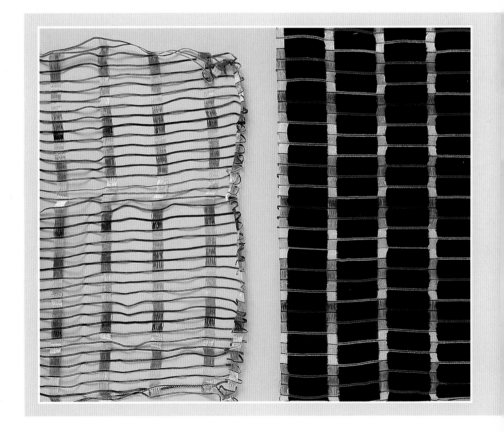

You can make your own open-weave fabric by knitting strips of China silk into a narrow rectangle of stockinette stitch. After knitting the desired length (before casting off), move the stitches to a circular needle. As you knit the last row, drop 1 to 3 stitches at intervals along the entire length of the knitting. When you pull the knitted fabric crosswise, the strands uncurl, forming a "ladder" or "run." Stretching the ladder taut, pin the fabric to your work surface and weave contrasting cotton strips through it.

# ALTERING THE WARP & WEFT STRIPS

An offer from Bonnie Berlin to share scraps from her embellished woven and quilted jacket triggered thoughts about reversible quilted yardage. Strips cut from quilted yardage are thicker and must have an edge treatment to cover the batting. Black synthetic suede proves to be a good companion because it is firm and heavy enough to pair with quilted strips, yet it remains flexible so the finished piece is not too stiff. Decorative stitches in rayon and metallic thread hide the raw edges of the cut strips as they hold the warp and weft together.

You can make a double-woven effect by weaving with strips of unquilted woven yardage. After tearing and pressing the weaving strips, apply a light coat of repositionable adhesive to the wrong side of each strip. Weave two panels of the desired size on top of a tulle foundation. (At this stage, tulle replaces the usual batting and backing, making the panel as lightweight as possible while holding it together for more cutting and weaving.) Cut each panel into 3"- to 4"-wide strips and carefully weave the strips on top of the usual batting and backing. Pin-baste well and quilt.

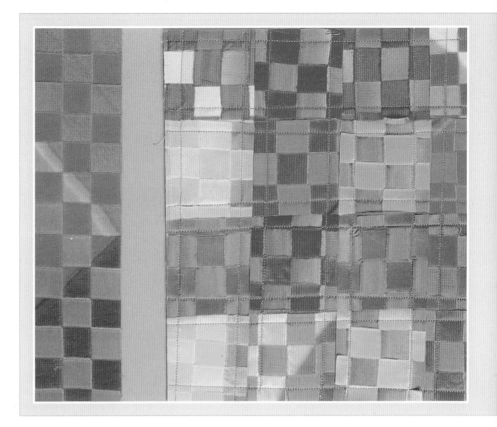

Create a visually dynamic surface with diagonal slits cut at random in the warp and weft strips. Thread narrow fabric strips of a contrasting color through the slits. As the strips cross over and under each other in a plain weave, the angles formed point the eye in different directions, leading the viewer over the entire plane.

You can change the width of a strip at intervals along its length by tearing it into narrower strips. For the illusion of a Nine Patch block framed by a postage-stamp border, begin with 3 warp strips and 2 weft strips, each 2" wide. Tear both ends of the strips into 4 equal widths, each 3" deep, making a fringe. Then, cut 4 slits, each 3" long, in the center of the middle warp strip. Tear 20 warp and weft strips, each ½" wide. Lay the warp in order: 4 narrow, 3 wide, 4 narrow. Weave the weft in order: 4 narrow, 1 wide, 4 narrow, 1 wide, 4 narrow.

During the weaving process, manipulate the warp or weft strips for a three-dimensional surface texture. Plan this type of special effect for small, removable areas of a garment to allow for easier cleaning. For a twill weave formed by rows of small bows, twist a light and dark strip together, tying a knot as the weft crosses the second warp strip. In the sample, the light print strip hides under the dark weft, showing only on top of the overhand knot. Decorative star stitches anchor the weft strips.

For another three-dimensional effect, machine stitch long, meandering basting lines (3 to 5 stitches per inch) down the center of a warp strip before weaving. While weaving, gather the strip tightly as it crosses the first weft, then allow it to lie flat as it goes under the next weft. Separate the gathered warp rows with several ungathered warp rows.

# WEAVING WITH MORE THAN TWO ELEMENTS

For a real challenge, consider triaxial weaving. One vertical and two diagonal strips intertwine in the sample to form a visual three-dimensional effect. Try the open-weave version (near right) first to practice the sequence of laying the strips, then move on to the more difficult closed weave (far right). Your choice of colors in light, medium, and dark values will emphasize the Baby Blocks pattern that results. Refer to the bibliography on page 87 for references on triaxial weaving.

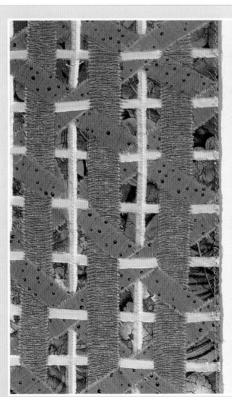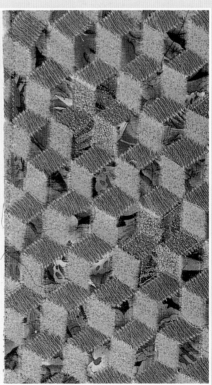

## CHAPTER 8

# Weaving Patterns

The colors and arrangement of your woven fabric strips create a design on the surface of your garment. Quilting lines enhance this visual and physical texture by adding areas of low relief. You can choose to highlight one of these elements or coordinate all three, for example, by repeating lines and shapes from the fabric surface in the weaving and quilting patterns.

In "Making Color Work for You" on page 6, you learned a little about color selection for woven and quilted garments. In this chapter, we look at the role of color in the woven structure and how color choice can define a weaving pattern or create another design unrelated to the weaving pattern. Examples of traditional weaving patterns in black and white and in color show you some options for each structure. Consider these samples as a guide for further exploration and take some time to experiment on your own.

You can get ideas for your woven and quilted wearables from traditional weaving patterns, with some modifications. Table looms and floor looms have heddles attached to harnesses that raise and lower many warp threads together. Weaving patterns are often identified according to the number of harnesses used, from two to sixty-four and beyond. For the woven and quilted process in this book, at first you might consider only patterns for two harnesses, since they seem easy, but that's an unnecessary limitation.

To determine whether you can adapt a traditional weaving pattern, look at a diagram of the surface instead of counting the number of harnesses. Patterns that have long floats (unsecured areas of a strip) can be used because the final quilting will hold the strips in place. Raising one warp strip at a time with your fingers or a needle, as in the woven and quilted process described in this book, gives you maximum flexibility in moving the weft across the warp.

The most obvious difference in weaving with fabric strips is a change in scale. A pattern designed to be woven with thin yarns will look quite different when magnified into giant-size with fabric strips. A structure that depends on many repeats of a small motif to establish the rhythm may lose its focus. Conversely, a monotonous surface might become intriguing when only a small amount of the repeat is shown.

The weaving patterns in this chapter offer some possibilities for your woven and quilted wearables. The patterns are divided into categories based on the relationship of the warp and weft to each other.

Each weaving pattern is given in black and white to show the basic structure. Subsequent examples demonstrate the dramatic way that color placement can move the focal point across the surface. Look closely at the illustrations and then gather your fabrics, tear them into strips, and work through the sample patterns to gain an understanding of the process.

## PLAIN WEAVES

Plain weaves are the most basic of all weaves—a simple repeat of over one, under one. Hopsack and basket weave are the same as plain weave, but you work with two yarns together. Like a plain baked potato, plain weaves are infinitely versatile. Changing the color, the width, or the shape of the strips will produce remarkably different designs.

# Tabby

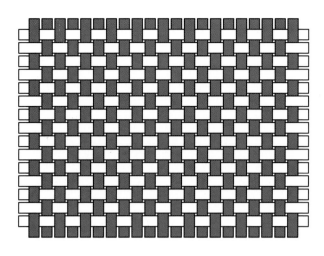 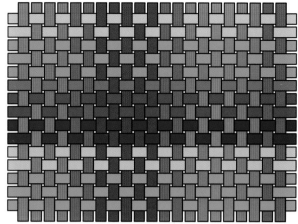

# Basket

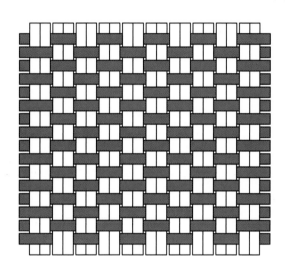 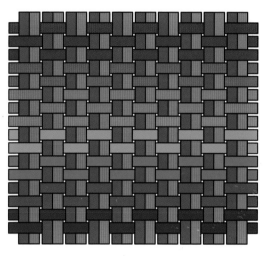

# Hopsack

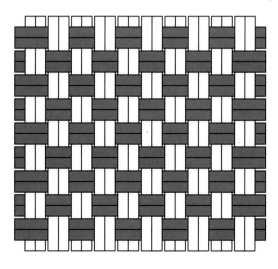 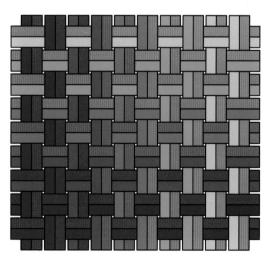

# Twill Weaves

Twill weaves feature distinct diagonals formed by the warp and weft floats. You can control the diagonals to move from left to right, from right to left, or in a zigzag pattern. The weft strips can cross over and under any number of warp strips to make a repeating design.

## Straight

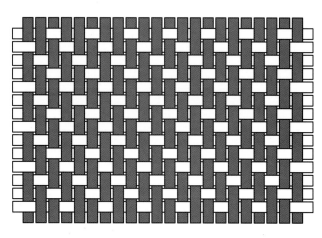 

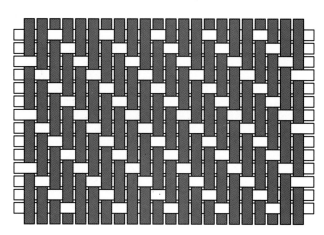 

## Herringbone

 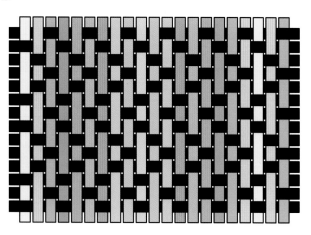

# *Offset*

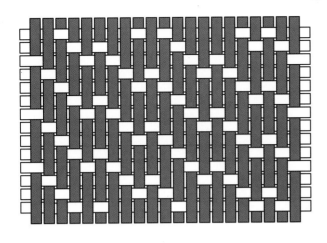 

# NOVELTY WEAVES

Novelty weaves, based on either a plain or twill structure, feature strips that are woven in a random manner or spread on a background. You may also change the width and shape of the individual strips for variation.

## *Warp and Weft of Different Widths*

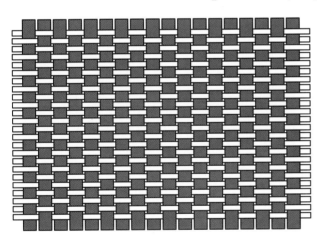 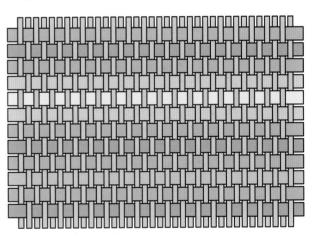

 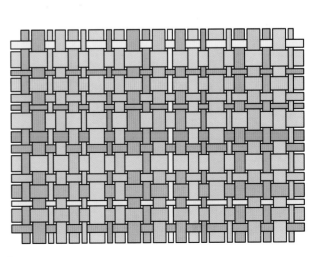

## Open

## Random

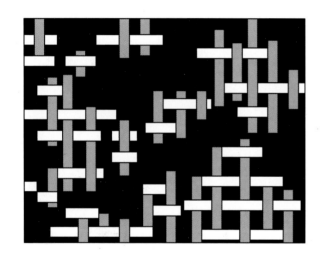

## Shaped Warp and Weft

# WEAVES WITH SPECIAL EFFECTS

Special effects include weaves that have the focus on the color or surface pattern of the fabric. The color effects are ma- nipulated, independent of the weaving structure, by arranging warp or weft strips of different colors in orderly repeats.

## Stripes

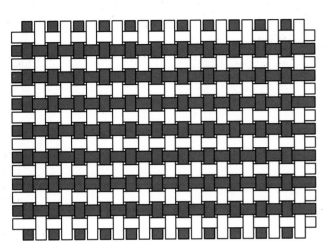

## Plaids

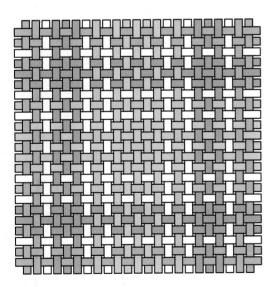
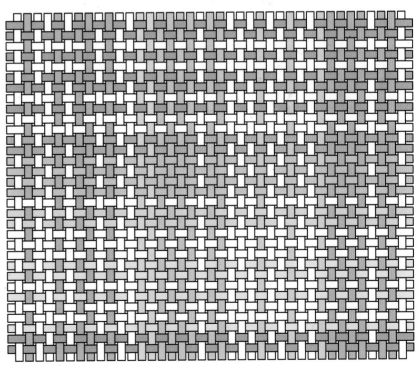

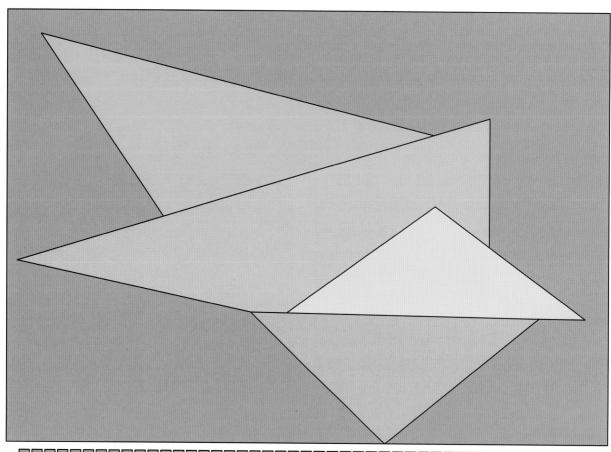

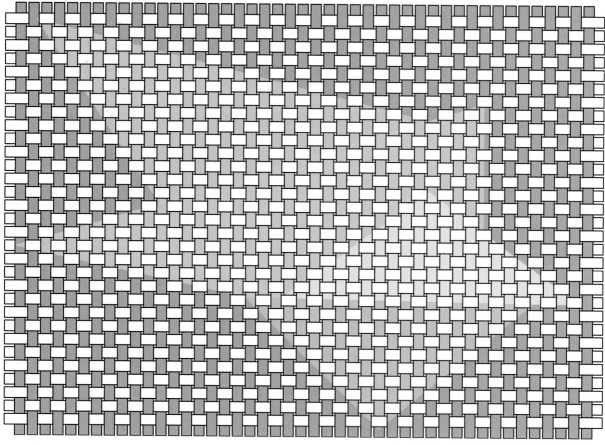

# Framing a Motif

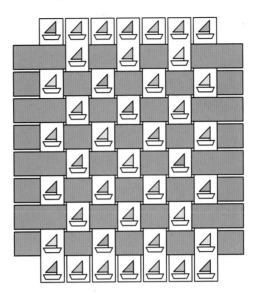

# Color and Weave

# Appendix

## Weaving Pattern Blanks

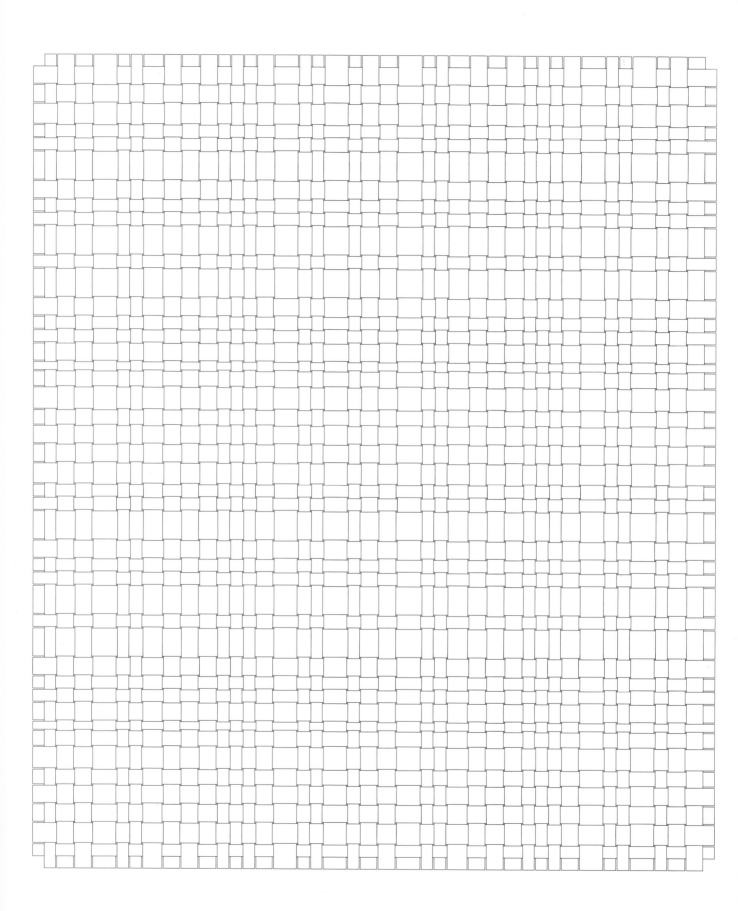

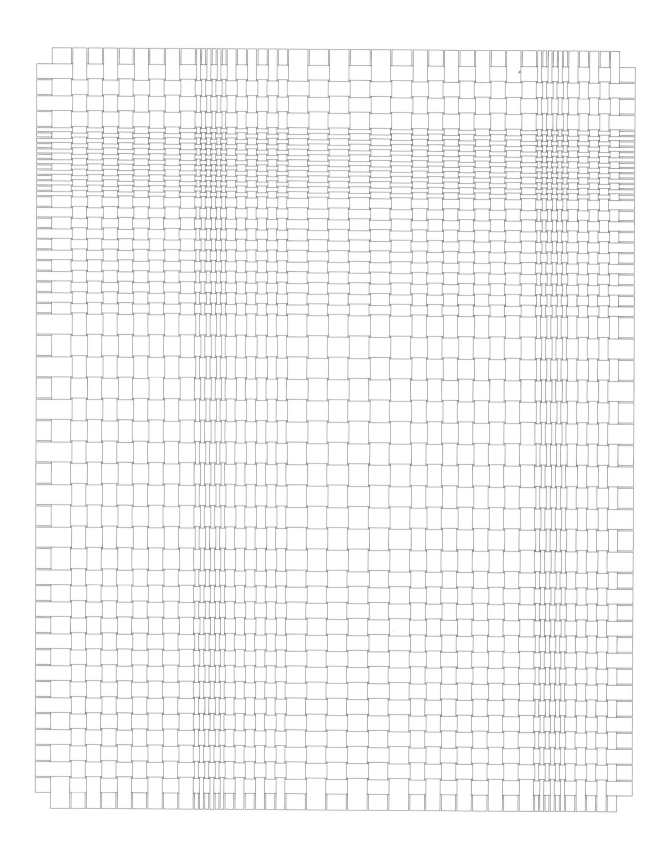

# SAMPLE VIEWFINDER SHAPES

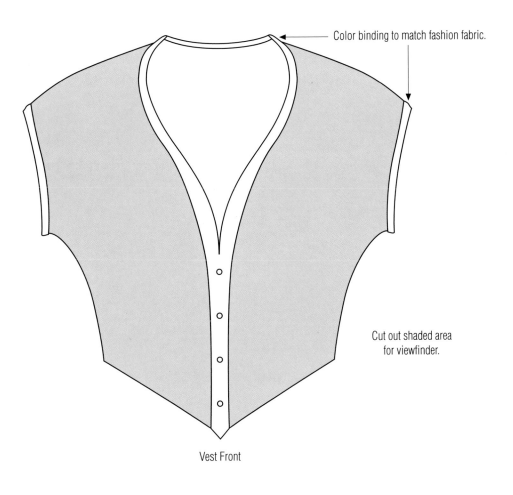

Color binding to match fashion fabric.

Cut out shaded area
for viewfinder.

Vest Front

Vest Back

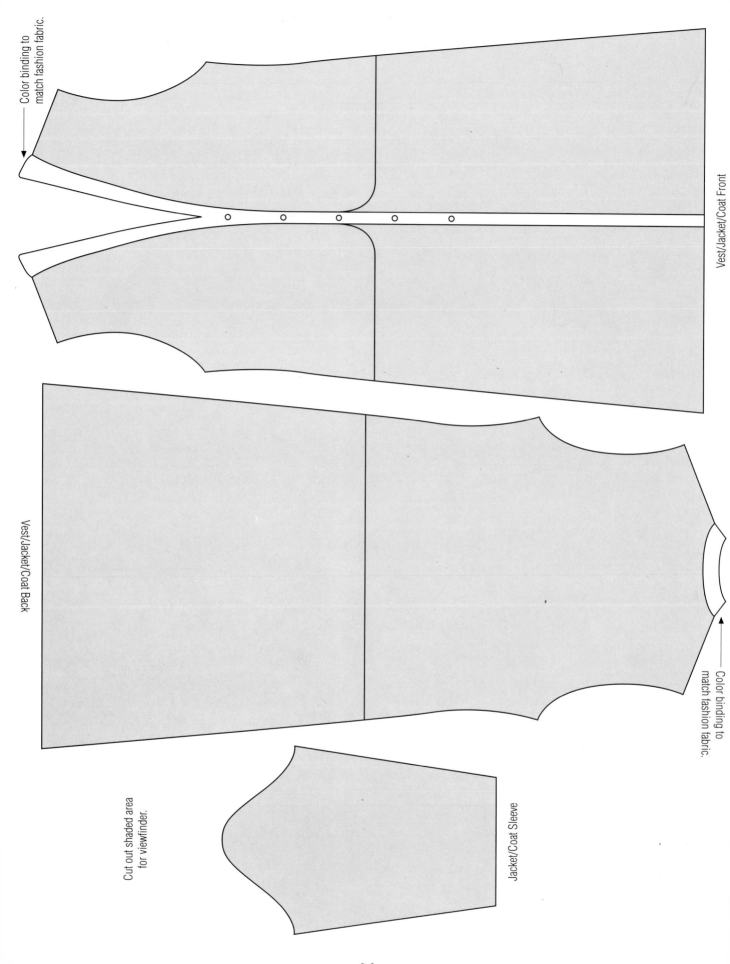

Color binding to
match fashion fabric.

Vest/Jacket/Coat Front

Vest/Jacket/Coat Back

Color binding to
match fashion fabric.

Cut out shaded area
for viewfinder.

Jacket/Coat Sleeve

# BIBLIOGRAPHY

Brown, Gail, Sue Green, and Pati Palmer. *Creative Serging*. Portland, Oreg.: Palmer/Pletsch Associates, 1987.

Brown, Gail, and Pati Palmer. *Sewing with Sergers*. Portland, Oreg.: Palmer/Pletsch Associates, 1985.

Caplinger, Mary Anne. *Woven and Quilted*. Bothell, Wash.: That Patchwork Place, 1995.

Fanning, Robbie, and Tony Fanning, *The Complete Book of Machine Quilting*, 2nd ed. Radnor, Pa.: Chilton Book Co., 1994.

Harvey, Virginia I. *The Techniques of Basketry*. Seattle, Wash.: University of Washington Press, 1988. (This book includes information on triaxial weaving.)

Jackson, Carole. *Color Me Beautiful*. New York: Ballantine Books, 1980.

LaPlantz, Shereen. *The Mad Weave Book*. Bayside, Calif.: Press de LaPlantz, 1984. (This book includes information on triaxial weaving and is available from Mary T. Klotz, Forestheart Studio, 200 South Main Street, Box 112, Woodsboro, MD 21798.)

Larkey, Jan. *Flatter Your Figure*. New York: Prentice Hall Press, 1991.

Marano, Hara Estroff. *Style Is Not a Size*. New York: Bantam Books, 1991.

McGurn, Linda M. "Knit One, Weave Two," *Threads* (May 1994): 70–73.

Noble, Maurine. *Machine Quilting Made Easy*. Bothell, Wash.: That Patchwork Place, 1994.

*The Perfect Fit: Singer Sewing Series*. Minnetonka, Minn.: Cy de Cosse, Inc., 1987.

Rasband, Judith. *Fabulous Fit*. New York: Fairchild Publications, 1994.

*The Serger Idea Book*. Portland, Oreg.: Palmer/Pletsch Associates, 1989.

Weiland, Barbara, and Leslie Wood. *Clothes Sense*. Portland, Oreg.: Palmer/Pletsch Associates, 1984.

Windeknecht, Margaret B. *Color-and-Weave II*. Rochester Hills, Mich: T. G. Windeknecht, 1994.

# RESOURCES

*Collapsible Cardboard Cutting Table*
Sew/Fit Company
PO Box 565
LaGrange, IL 60525

*Work-Space Board*
Keepsake Quilting
Route 25
PO Box 1618
Centre Harbor, NH 03226-1618
(603) 253-8731

*Poppanna Yarn*
Eaton Yarns
PO Box 665
Tarrytown, NY 10591
(914) 631-1550

*Batik Fabric*
Batiks, Etc.
411 Pine Street
Fort Mill, SC
800/BATIKS-ETC

*Double Mirror*
Clotilde, Inc.
2 Sew Smart Way, B8031
Stevens Point, WI 54481-8031
800/772-2891

# MEET THE AUTHOR

Mary Anne Caplinger's love of fiber was a heritage passed down from her mother and grandmothers. "As soon as my mother felt comfortable with it, I had a needle in my hand," she says. "According to her, my second word was scissors."

Over the years, as she realized the creative possibilities inherent in cloth, Mary Anne began experimenting with a variety of textile structures and surface-design techniques. Today, she devotes her time and creative energies to fabric painting, dyeing, silk-screen printing, and stamping. She hand dyes almost all the fabrics she uses in her weaving.

Mary Anne has been making and exhibiting quilts and quilted wearables since 1973. As a balance to the long hours spent working alone, she enjoys teaching quilting and surface design to quilters in the Southeast. When she's not working with fabric, Mary Anne likes to read, garden, and travel.

Native Midwesterners, Mary Anne and her husband, John, now live in Wilkesboro, North Carolina, where they are both active in the local community. They are the parents of two grown children.

# Publications and Products

---

4", 6", 8" & metric Bias Square® • BiRangle™
Ruby Beholder® • ScrapMaster • Rotary Rule™
Rotary Mate™ • Bias Stripper®
Shortcuts to America's Best-Loved Quilts (video)

---

Many titles are available at your local quilt shop.
For more information, send $2 for a color catalog to
That Patchwork Place, Inc., PO Box 118, Bothell,
WA 98041-0118 USA.

☎ U.S. and Canada, call **1-800-426-3126** for the
name and location of the quilt shop nearest you.
Int'l: 1-206-483-3313   Fax: 1-206-486-7596
E-mail: info@patchwork.com
Web: http://oak.forest.net/patchwork       6.96